TWAYNE'S WORLD AUTHORS SERIES

A Survey of the World's Literature

Sylvia E. Bowman, Indiana University

GENERAL EDITOR

SPAIN

Gerald Wade, Vanderbilt University

EDITOR

Dolores Medio

(TWAS 281)

TWAYNE'S WORLD AUTHORS SERIES (TWAS)

The purpose of TWAS is to survey the major writers—novelists, dramatists, historians, poets, philosophers, and critics—of the nations of the world. Among the national literatures covered are those of Australia, Canada, China, Eastern Europe, France, Germany, Greece, India, Italy, Japan, Latin America, the Netherlands, New Zealand, Poland, Russia, Scandinavia, Spain, and the African nations, as well as Hebrew, Yiddish, and Latin Classical literature. This survey is complemented by Twayne's United States Authors Series and English Authors Series.

The intent of each volume in these series is to present a critical-analytical study of the works of the writer; to include biographical and historical material that may be necessary for understanding, appreciation, and critical appraisal of the writer; and to present all material in clear, concise English—but not to vitiate the scholarly content of the work by doing so.

Dolores Medio

By Margaret E. W. Jones

University of Kentucky

Twayne Publishers, Inc. :: New York

PQ
6623
.E 42
Z 73

ISBN-0-8057-2610-1

To Alison Margaret

Preface

This book attempts to introduce Dolores Medio to the American public. Her first novel, *Nosotros los Rivero (We Riveros)* was responsible for her meteoric rise to fame as well as for a full-fledged polemic over its relative merits, which most Spanish reviewers found old-fashioned and sentimental. Perhaps as a result of these objections, she has evolved a style which now pleases most of the critics. It is this evolution and the reason behind the change that are of interest to the student of contemporary literature, for this new philosophy is typical of the work of a whole generation of writers no longer preoccupied with the aesthetics of art for art's sake.

Miss Medio represents a group of writers who are concerned with the problems of contemporary society: social conditions, economic hardships, the movement from the city to the country, the lack of understanding between the classes. Their collective style tends to be "realistic," but this does not preclude experimental techniques to enhance the message. Yet Miss Medio does not write literature for propaganda purposes. On the contrary, her intense interest in the individual, the warmth and sympathy with which she develops the human elements in the stories, raise the works to a level that includes the universal application along with the specific.

An introductory chapter will present a brief survey of major themes in the contemporary Spanish novel. Its purpose is to signal major directions in the novel today and place Dolores Medio within the framework of current trends.

The biographical information will show how much of Miss Medio's experiences have found their way into fiction. Several of her heroines are alter egos who are quite like the author herself: unmarried, a writer or a teacher, an independent person who is keenly observant of human foibles and also tolerant of them.

I have approached the task of presenting Miss Medio's work through literary analysis supplemented heavily with biographical facts, for her extraliterary point of view must also be taken into consideration. Her theory of personality formation, for example, influenced by Normal School training and studies in psychological development, has been applied directly to her characters, whom she often treats as case studies. Thus it is essential to elucidate the connection between life and literature. This will be accomplished in a first chapter devoted to biographical information and literary theory. Subsequent chapters will contain references to her opinions and experiences as these appear in her fiction.

The main consideration in this study has been given to the author's fictional works. Each of her novels has its own chapter; the shorter fiction is grouped into two separate chapters, a division necessitated by a chronological separation as well as by Miss Medio's technical and ideological development. The nonfiction is considered more briefly in the last chapter; although the biographies of Isabel II and Selma Lagerlöf and the guidebook of Asturias illustrate the consistency of her point of view, they are given less space in this book because Miss Medio feels that her greatest successes have been in the area of prose fiction, that she is primarily a novelist rather than an essayist, and for this reason, one with which I agree, her nonfictional work requires less attention in a book like this one.

An integral part of these chapters are brief passages which illustrate the writer's style or emphasize certain ideas. I am responsible for the translations; wherever possible I have followed the text exactly, but at times it has been necessary to deviate from literal translation in order to impart the intention or mood. Page numbers in parentheses will follow the quotations.

Miss Medio has a wealth of unpublished material in varying stages of completion as well as a number of poems, stories, etc., published in obscure periodicals or newspapers. She has supplied me with copies of this work whenever possible. I have decided, however, to concentrate on published materials which are easily accessible to the reader of this book, supplementing the materials, whenever appropriate, with references to the unpublished manuscripts.

Dolores Medio is an active writer and continues to produce at a fast pace. At the time of this writing, one book *(La otra circunstancia)* is in press; three others are in varying stages of completion and will be published in the near future. It is a pleasant task to present what this author has published, to point out themes and stylistic traits which are typical, and to emphasize the continuing concerns which have marked Miss Medio's work to date and which, presumably, will continue to provide the basis of her literature and her popularity with her public.

Contents

Chronology

1914   Dolores Medio born in Oviedo. The beginning of World War I; Spain remains neutral.

1921   Miss Medio studies music and drawing at the Escuela de Bellas Artes.

1923   Beginning of the dictatorship of Primo de Rivera.

1926   Miss Medio writes her first novel, *Egoismo (Selfishness)*, which remains unpublished.

1927   Her father dies; the family loses the family business and lives in very reduced circumstances.

1928   Miss Medio attends Normal School to prepare for a teaching career.

1930   The Rivera dictatorship ends.

1931   The Second Republic proclaimed; elections won by Republican-Socialist alliance.

1933   The *Cortes* dissolved; elections put Rightists in power.

1934   The uprising in Asturias. Violent suppression by the government.

1936   New elections won by the Popular Front and marked by more violence and bloodshed. Civil war begins. Miss Medio begins her teaching career at Nava (near Oviedo) and is almost immediately relieved of the position because of distrust of the new pedagogical methods. Her mother dies during the war.

1939   The end of the Civil War; victory for Franco's Nationalist forces.

1940   Miss Medio is allowed to resume teaching.

1945   She wins the Concha Espina Prize for short story "Nina." Moves to Madrid, studies Pedagogy and Journalism. Begins work on the paper *El Domingo*.

1948   Publishes the children's book *El milagro de la Noche de Reyes (The Miracle of Epiphany Eve)*.

1953   Wins the Nadal Prize for the novel *Nosotros los Rivero (We Riveros)*.

1954   Publishes *Compás de espera (Pause)* and *Mañana (Tomorrow)*.

1956   Publication of *Funcionario público (Public Servant)*.

1959   *El pez sigue flotando (The Fish Stays Afloat)* is published.

1961   Publication of *Diario de una maestra (Diary of a Schoolteacher)*.

1962   Miss Medio is jailed for one month for being present at a women's demonstration, although she did not take part. She writes *Celda común (Prison Ward)*, unpublished at present because of censorship, about the women she met in prison.

1963   Publication of *Bibiana*, the first part of the trilogy *Los que vamos a pie (We Who Go on Foot)*.

1965   *El Domingo* stops publication without notice. Miss Medio sues the publisher and wins, receiving a small indemnification.

1966   Publication of *El señor García (Mr. García* and *Isabel II,* a biography.

1967   Miss Medio publishes *Andrés*, for which she wins the Sésamo short-story prize.

1971   She publishes *Asturias*, a guidebook, and *Selma Lagerlöf*, a biography.

CHAPTER 1

The Post-Civil War Spanish Novel:
A Thematic Prospect

THE vacuum of high quality literature following the Spanish Civil War (1936–1939) was filled by two works which reflected the violent attitude characteristic of the depression of the period. They were Camilo José Cela's *La familia de Pascual Duarte (The Family of Pascual Duarte)*, 1942, and Carmen Laforet's *Nada (Nothing)*, 1945. Both are representative in tone of the first of the artistic *-isms* to follow the war: *tremendismo*, a literary movement characterized by physical and mental violence and anguish, doubtless a symbolic reflection of conditions in Spain at the time of writing. The basic (though at times distorted) realism of these two works has set the tone of prevalent stylistic trends in the Spanish novel for the following decades, although the thematics have changed to reflect the spirit of the moment. Perhaps the stringent restrictions on the diffusion of foreign books hampered familiarity with influences which would have encouraged literary experimentation, and this may account for the continuance of the tradition of Realism which critics have cited as one of the constants of the Spanish outlook. Whatever the reasons, this "characteristic" realism has been updated to enhance contemporary themes, many of them acidly critical of prevailing national or universal conditions. A description of this variety is one way of approaching the complex problem of the contemporary Spanish novel, for the subjects mentioned below find their way into the works of the majority of present-day Spanish writers with varying degrees of emphasis. Of special interest to this study is the fact that Dolores Medio, too, has made liberal use of most of these themes in her own works.[1]

I   Literary Traditions: Continuation and Revival

The adaptation of traditional forms of Realism has never wanted in popularity, and many writers have begun their careers with works which reflect techniques of the Spanish nineteenth-century novel. They have as common themes the interaction of the individual with the society in which he lives, and often depict the social or political pressures or historical events which shape the destiny of the protagonists. Miss Medio's *Nosotros los Rivero (We Riveros)* falls into this category, as does Ignacio Agustí's *Mariona Rebull* (1944) and many of Juan Antonio de Zunzunegui's novels.

A collateral branch of the traditional novel is the rural or regional work, which may have as its remote ancestor the *artículo de costumbres*. One sees an emphasis on the special qualities of the region— its costumes, speech patterns, way of life, special attitudes; in short, things that provide distinguishing factors. These characteristics, however, move at times from a place of primary importance to background material, often for social themes. Angel María de Lera's *La boda (The Wedding)*, 1959, is one example.

Although the adherence to patterns of traditional Realism is simply an unbroken continuation of a literary form, quite noteworthy is the revival of older modes of Spanish literature. The picaresque novel has been adapted by various writers: Camilo José Cela's *Nuevas andanzas y desventuras de Lazarillo de Tormes (New Sallies and Misadventures of Lazarillo de Tormes)*, 1944, is unmistakable in its inspiration; still other works have the flavor of the picaresque: Zunzunegui's *El Chiplechandle (The Ship's Chandler)*, 1940, or *La vida como es (Life Like it Is)*, 1950. Ana María Matute's *La torre vigía (The Watchtower)*, 1971, shows the influence of the medieval chivalric novel. The special types of literature cultivated by the Generation of 1898 (the literary group which included Unamuno, Baroja, Valle-Inclán, and Azorín, among others) have also heavily influenced the younger writers. Baroja has inspired several works; the form of the *esperpento* (Valle-Inclán's definition of a literary form which presents society— specifically Spain—through a concave mirror, because "Spain is a grotesque deformation of European civilization") finds its way into the contemporary novel to a greater or lesser degree in some of the more grotesque episodes (in the novels of Cela or Ana María Matute, for example).

The revival of the nineteenth-century historical novel recalls other traditions in Spanish literature. Such works may recreate remote times (the works of Alejandro Núñez Alonso concerning the Roman era), Spain's history (Ramón Sender's *La aventura equinoccial de Lope de Aguirre (The Equinoctial Adventure of Lope de Aguirre*, 1964*)*, the more immediate past (the nineteenth century in Ignacio Agustí's *Mariona Rebull*), or novels concerning the Civil War. Ricardo Fernández de la Reguera and Susana March are currently producing a series of *Episodios nacionales contemporáneos*, beginning with 1898.

The related novel of the Civil War is the literary expression of the most immediate reality following the disaster. A popular protagonist is the individual who is caught up in the war but cannot comprehend what is happening to him; Fernández de la Reguera's *Cuerpo a tierra (Hit the Dirt)*, 1954, or Ana María Matute's *En esta tierra (In This Land)*, 1955, are two examples. Commentaries on human nature use the war as background or catalyst (Ramón Sender's *El rey y la reina* [*The King and the Queen*], 1947, or *Mossén Millan*, 1953). José María Gironella's trilogy describes the Civil War through a panoramic view of society and government; these works include the popular *Los cipreses creen en Dios (The Cypresses Believe in God)*, 1953, *Un millón de muertos (A Million Dead)*, 1961, and *Ha estallado la paz (Peace has Broken Forth)*, 1960. The Civil War continues to provide a theme which writers explore with ever-renewed interest and depth. Cela's *Vísperas, festividad, y octava de San Camilo del año 1936 en Madrid (Eve, Festivity and Octave of St. Camillus' Day, 1936, in Madrid)*, 1969, is a recent product of this trend.

II   *New Symbols*

The modern reconstruction of the Cain-Abel fratricide can also be considered a direct result of the search for symbols worthy of the Civil War. It is a constant in the works of Ana María Matute (her first published novel was called *Los Abel* [*The Abel Family*]); her other works implicitly or explicitly develop the theme. Juan Goytisolo's *Duelo en el Paraíso (Mourning in Paradise)*, 1955, describes the sacrifice of a boy named Abel.

Books about children also form a special grouping which offers universal as well as national implications. The innocence of childhood is often shattered by an event which indicates man's evil nature *(Primera memoria* [*First Memories*], 1960, by Matute). Children's imitative faculties provide a horror story in *Mourning in Paradise*, in which children in a refugee camp mimic adult violence. Both Matute and Goytisolo were children during the Civil War, and with others of their generation they generally view childhood with a sense of loss of innocence, and point to man's corruptible nature viewed in microcosmic form through children. Significantly, older writers treat childhood as a kind of mythical Paradise before the Fall; in this case innocence contrasts with the guilty adult (Ramón Sender's *Crónica del alba* [*Chronicle of the Dawn*], 1942; Miguel Delibes' *El camino* [*The Road*], 1950).

Adolescence offers the writer another means to air his views. As a manner of protest, many adolescents rebel against what they consider outmoded social forms. Such defiance of the Establishment may take the form of murder, as in Juan Goytisolo's *Juegos de manos* (*Sleight of Hand*), 1954; of gratuitous self-sacrifice, as in Matute's *Los soldados lloran de noche* (*Soldiers Cry in the Night*), 1964, or of the feeling of total alienation from one's environment (Laforet's *Nothing*). In the case of both childhood and adolescence, the process of maturation may include an abrupt change from one age to another, often a symbolic rite of passage with its concomitant traumatic experience.

III   The Novel as Vehicle for Criticism

Social criticism has grown in intensity during the post-Civil War period. Specific situations which suggest necessary reforms are described in almost documentary fashion. The emigration from southern Spain to the northern regions and its socioeconomic problems is presented in *La mina* (*The Mine*), 1960, by Armando López Salinas, and is a secondary theme in *Fiestas* (1958) by Juan Goytisolo. *Hemos perdido el sol* (*We Have Lost the Sun*), 1965, by Angel María de Lera, describes the situation of the Spanish emigrant worker in Germany. Works like *Central eléctrico* (*Powerhouse*), 1958, by Jesús López Pacheco picture the impact of a big business venture on a backward rural area. Realistic descriptions of contemporary life appear in many novels, among them Dolores Medio's *Funcionario público* (*Public Servant*), 1953, and Antonio Ferres' *La piqueta* (*The Pickaxe*), 1959. They have a common interest in their critical intention and their portrayal of the protagonist as victim of forces beyond his control (a company, social or economic pressures, etc.).

It is inevitable that economic or social forces at play in Spain today should determine the subject matter of its literature. The access of easy money and its influence on the younger generation, the great influx of tourism, the sudden prosperity in certain regions (especially in the south of Spain) have inspired several novels about the idle rich, the "vacation crowd," and the *dolce vita*. Among these are Juan Goytisolo's *La isla (The Island)*, 1961, and José María Sanjuan's *Requiem por todos nosotros (Requiem for Us All)*, 1968. A different, but no less effective type of criticism focuses on "the problem of Spain." This subject has been of vital interest since the eighteenth century and has gained in impetus since that time, culminating in the literary formalization of the theme with the Generation of 1898. No doubt because of the direct influence of this famous group of writers, the contemporary novel shows a tendency toward the same kind of self-examination: a disenchantment with Spain and her institutions, a focus on the less desirable features of her people: abulia, stubbornness, cruelty, hypocrisy, ignorance. In addition, modern writers have emphasized the more contemporary themes of dehumanization and alienation. Surely the most outstanding example in the novel is the innovational *Tiempo de silencio (Time of Silence)*, 1961, by Luis Martín-Santos. Using a combination of existential psychoanalysis, experimental techniques which embrace such diverse influences as English literature, mythology, the Spanish Baroque, and Pío Baroja, this work is a scathing indictment of social, economic, and moral conditions of present-day Spain. Martín-Santos' untimely death truncated what surely would have been a brilliant literary career. Another critical work with an innovational style is Miguel Delibes' *Parábola del náufrago (Parable of the Drowning Man)*, 1969, in which the protagonist is forced to conform in order to survive; dehumanization of present conditions finally turns him into a sheep who forms part of the flock. Still other examples of specific criticism of Spanish conditions and mentality are two works of Juan Goytisolo published outside of Spain: *Señas de identidad (Signs of Identity)*, 1966, and *Reivindicación del conde don Julián*, 1970.

There is a fine line between criticism of specifically Spanish institutions and criticism of human nature as seen through Spanish eyes and in Spanish conditions. Many of Cela's works fall into the second category, although they are unmistakably Spanish in setting.

IV   *Literary Experimentation, Continuing Preoccupations*

Cela's work also tends toward experimentation: *La colmena (The Hive)*, 1951, uses a multiple protagonist to expose man's basic selfishness and cruelty. The myriad characters in this work are even greater in his *Tobagán de hambrientos* (*Toboggan of Hungry People*), 1962, which provides a similar perspective, using cruelty, disenchantment, and alienation as common denominators. Many of Ana María Matute's works may be viewed in this same ambivalent category: universal themes of hypocrisy, cruelty, alienation, noncommunication take place on a specifically Spanish level. Thus her trilogy *Los mercaderes* (*The Moneychangers*) moves from a general sense of isolation during the Civil War (it is set on an island) in *First Memories,* to a specific form of protest during the fighting itself (*Soldiers Cry in the Night,* 1964) to a final tragic episode set during the present, but triggered by a motive of revenge connected with Civil War (*La trampa* [*The Trap*], 1969).

The search for Spain's essence often was a physical as well as a mental process for the Generation of 1898; Baroja, especially, had his protagonists wander through Castile (the heart and soul of Spain) in search of themselves. Although Castile and its people are still the background of novels (in several works of Jesús Fernández Santos or Ana María Matute), there has developed another subgenre, closely related to the novel, but which must be called quasifiction: the travel books. Cela started the trend, which has gained quickly in popularity. Often written in the third person, but in diary form, the "wanderer" (Cela) travels through various regions—Castile, northern Spain, Andalusia—relating history, personal anecdotes, descriptions of the places and the people; in short, a mixture of objective and subjective writing which offers a panoramic view of the Spanish spirit. His first travel book, *Viaje a la Alcarria* (*Trip to the Alcarria Region*), 1948, is a typical example: the people seem subservient, with inferiority complexes, and look to the past rather than the future for inspiration. Cela has continued to produce travel books about Spain; others, like Juan Goytisolo, have followed suit. A recent manifestation of this is the commentary on the novelist's travels abroad; Lera, Laforet, Delibes, and Castillo Puche are among the many who describe their reactions to a foreign culture.

Cela's *The Hive* and *Toboggan of Hungry People* are indicative of another trend in style which most effectively mirrors the content of the work. The use of the multiple character rather than the single hero or antihero suggests a new thematic approach to the novel. The idea of the collectivity thus becomes much stronger, and the rapid movement from one incident to another gives the impression of a cross-section of life which may provide a rich in-depth view of society. Other authors, including Dolores Medio *(El pez sigue flotando [The Fish Stays Afloat])*, have developed this technique to great advantage. In this case, the subject arises naturally from the special form.

There are other instances in which form and content are interwoven to a great degree. The *novela objetivista*, in vogue during the past two decades, proclaims a greater objectivity through the elimination of psychological content and author intervention, with a phenomenalist approach to the data at hand (visual, auditory, surface structures). Although *The Hive* may be considered an early manifestation of this movement (the multiple episodes are viewed as so many snapshots, with the author in the role of an "arranger"), the most outstanding example must be *El Jarama*, by Rafael Sánchez Ferlosio (1956). Describing a Sunday on the shores of the Jarama River, this author simply "transcribes" the conversations and interactions of two groups: young people who have come from Madrid for a day's outing, and the group of regulars at Lucio's bar. The death of a young girl ends the day in tragedy. Sánchez Ferlosio has so accurately captured the speech patterns that he has been "accused" of taping conversations and simply transcribing them; quite an indirect compliment for this author's supposed pretensions toward objectivity. [2]

Form and content are often mutually dependent in the modern psychological novel, present in the form of diary or confession in a stream-of-consciousness technique through which the writer-subject probes into the depth of his being to discover subconscious motives or to elucidate some heretofore hidden aspect of his character. Both Elena Quiroga's *Algo pasa en la calle (Something Is Happening Outside)*, 1954, and Delibes' *Cinco horas con Mario (Five Hours with Mario)*, 1966, use a corpse to trigger the recollections, inspired by his life and death.

In general, the theme of alienation seems to be present in almost all postwar literature. Whether a universally modern current, or the result of the impact of the Civil War, the characters are often out of step with society, misunderstood by family and friends, and unable to communicate with others. Efforts to bridge the gap are generally unsuccessful, and the protagonist not only cannot succeed in his endeavor, but in addition has acquired the knowledge of his failure. Examples of psychological alienation or estrangement can be found in the works of Matute, Goytisolo, Delibes (both social and emotional), and, in varying degrees, in almost every novel produced in recent decades.

A brief survey such as this must necessarily limit itself to the most prevalent types in the contemporary Spanish novel. Other themes which have been developed in recent times would include the Catholic novel, the detective novel, the book of memoirs or reminiscences, and the popular *novela rosa* (sentimental novel), to mention only a few more.

V *The Current Situation*

Today's writer faces a series of challenges of an extraliterary nature which may well set some of the norms for writing itself. On the one hand, the many literary prizes offered today in Spain are attractive and at times lucrative (among them, the prestigious Premio Eugenio Nadal, the Premio Planeta, the Premio Nacional de Literatura). These awards have launched many a young writer or confirmed the fame of a more established one. However, the censorship practiced in Spain discourages the exploration of controversial or politically delicate areas. Even the supposed relaxation in censorship laws has not offered complete freedom to the writer; it has changed the criteria in such a way as to provide a strange post facto publication rule. One novelist describes the recent change in the following way: "As for political factors, they are exactly those which restrain any written expression of opinion in Spain. Until very recently, at times of greater or lesser severity, Spanish writers suffered a tasteless, anonymous, frivolous and contradictory antecedent censorship capable of condemning to ostracism without appeal a book which, three months later, might be mysteriously authorized in its entirety. At present, we profit from a new modality, much more tortuous. In key with the new, peculiar, and unexpected democratic sentiment, we may publish anything—very well, almost anything—without the necessity of consulting an antecedent censorship. Censorship may come later, as narrow, arbitrary, and inconsistent as circumstances then warrant. *After* publication may come the confiscation of a book by the police, suppression of a magazine, the exorbitant fine, perhaps trial and prison."[3]

Despite this factor, Spain has produced some excellent literature in recent decades, and is receiving a place of deserved recognition in the field of contemporary letters. In part, an increase in translations is responsible for the wider diffusion of Spanish literature. Of more importance, however, is the writer's interest in mankind in general, striking common chords which involve readers outside of his own country. The ability to identify or empathize with the themes in the contemporary Spanish novel has given it a wider sphere of influence and a greater range of readers.

CHAPTER 2

Experience as Artistic Raw Material

DOLORES Medio is part of a generation of novelists who, in general, practice a literary realism with social implications. This type of literature may range in style and content from the simple, journalistic presentation of a situation with social, ethical, or moral import to imitations of the French New Novel, with its elimination of authorial intervention and psychological content. Although she does indeed share some of these concerns and attitudes, Miss Medio nevertheless does not always lend herself to easy categorization, for autobiographical and personal elements in her novels often individualize much of her own work, and thus put on it a distinctive stamp that removes her from any "school" of literary practitioners. It is, then, prudent to view her literature in the light of her own biography and social milieu, for she has drawn heavily on episodes in her own life and on the characteristics of a class and an ambiance with which she is thoroughly familiar. Her experiences, elaborated artistically, are then transmitted to her readers as a fictionalized reality.

Miss Medio has been very helpful in providing information about herself, her literary and personal preferences, and has not hesitated to offer refreshingly candid expressions of her opinions. With her own words, taken from correspondence and interviews, and with supplements from other sources, it is possible to formulate her biography in considerable detail.[1]

I The Early Years, 1914–1945

Dolores Medio was born in 1914 in Oviedo, the capital of Spain's northern province of Asturias. Her family was of the middle class. Her father, Ramón Medio-Tuya y Rivero, had led an exciting life of travel and adventure—his various professions included those of banker, colonist, soldier, merchant. On his final return to Spain he married one of the respectable young ladies of Oviedo, Maria Teresa Estrada y Pastor. As a child, Dolores worshipped her father, whose stories of his adventures offered an escape from prosaic reality. This close attachment soon ended; her father died when she was quite young, leaving an economic as well as an emotional vacuum in the Medio family. The bank foreclosed on their store and they were forced to move to a less desirable section of the city. The difference between the ways of life the family led before and after the father's death was indeed discouraging, for during his life they lived comfortably, perhaps at times extravagantly, but their new life was marked by extreme poverty. Dolores had to give up her studies of art and music—two great loves—and turn to a teaching career instead. To help with the family finances, she gave private lessons in elementary school subjects, concealing her age (she was then thirteen) by wearing high heels and glasses. She also made hand-painted toys and aided persons in filling out tax receipts after school hours. Miss Medio attributes her ability to survive during those difficult times to her inveterate optimism.

Dolores spent the summer months as a governess at the palatial home of the Marqués de Villaverde in Galicia. A precocious awareness of social inequities was born during this time. She could see the marked difference between the luxurious life of the upper class and the hardships of the laborers who worked for the family. She also was the object of class prejudice, looked down upon by the servants and ignored by her employers. Perhaps this helped to form her philosophy concerning the instability of the Spanish middle class, which she feels is isolated between two other social strata and which eventually will merge into one or the other and disappear.[2]

Dolores showed early signs of literary interest, composing short stories at the age of five and, four years later, creating a children's theater which presented plays that she herself had written. At twelve, she wrote her first long (unpublished) novel, *Egoísmo (Selfishness)*, a story which reveals some of the social pressures of the times. Based on an episode from her own family life, the novel refers to the self-interest of a mother who wants to marry her daughter into a good situation, regardless of the girl's feelings or preferences.

Dolores' early years were also difficult ones for Spain, and particularly in the northern regions. Her birth coincided with the first year of the First World War, "this terrible year for Humanity," to use the author's own words,[3] though Spain remained neutral. Alfonso XIII was king at the time, and the country was plagued with social and political problems. The governments which followed

in rapid succession (a military dictatorship; then the Second
Republic, with its radically opposed parties alternately in power)
did not improve conditions; intense struggles for political domi-
nance, efforts at reforms and counter-reforms gave the impression
of political chaos. Dissatisfaction with these and many other events
brought about an uprising in Asturias in 1934, fomented by Socialist
and labor groups. The suppressions that followed were characterized
by extreme violence on the part of the police and the soldiers, and
by atrocities on the part of the revolutionaries; one historian's
description of the revolutionary takeover of Oviedo mentions bom-
bings, looting, and burnings.[4] As the situation assumed frightening
proportions, a new election voted in the Popular Front, a coalition
of all the Republican parties, ranging in ideology from Socialist to
Anarchist. The reaction to this reelection was more violence:
killings and the destruction of churches marked the inauguration of
this administration.

The unstable situation, and especially the uprising in Asturias,
made a deep impression on Dolores, who personally witnessed much
of the action. The effects of the Second Republic and the Asturian
revolution are recorded in her first novel *Nosotros los Rivero*
(We Riveros), her most clearly autobiographical work. The disillusionment she suffered upon seeing the Republic crumble was
responsible for her formation of a new philosophy toward life
based on tolerance and comprehension of others, even though
one may not be in agreement with them. Although she believed
in the ideals of the Second Republic, she was shocked at the behavior
of the revolutionaries. Then she tried to understand the reason
behind their destructiveness, and came to the conclusion that the
intellectuals and the upper classes were to blame for not providing
the common people with an adequate education, with the inculcation
of moral principles that might have warded off some of the acts of
violence that were committed in 1934.

Dolores began her teaching career in the town of Nava, near
Oviedo, in 1936. There she applied some of the new methods she
learned in school: a progressive, ungraded educational system inspired by the American-born Dalton Laboratory Plan. The townspeople were suspicious of such a departure from tradition and
regarded the experiment as Marxist or Socialist. She was relieved
of her position in the same year. Since they could not find sufficient
legal cause for permanent dismissal, she was reinstated in 1940,

but was subject to several restrictions: she was not allowed to take the public examinations necessary for promotion, to hold any supervisory position, or to continue with her studies. However unfortunate her experiences in the teaching profession may have been, they contributed in large measure to her formation as a writer. She profited greatly by her studies (especially in psychology and philosophy) and from the observation of her pupils and their parents.

The Spanish Civil War (1936–1939) wrought havoc throughout the country and was marked by hatred and murder on both sides. Miss Medio did not escape the effects. Since the dismissal from her position left her with no references, she could not obtain employment in teaching or in any other job that required a recommendation. To keep alive, she worked at whatever she could find: in a bottling factory, as a maid, or filling out official documents. Although she was not affiliated with any political movement, she was detained several times for questioning by the authorities. Her personal and family life were also drastically affected: her mother died and her fiancé was killed during the war.

Miss Medio's observations of wartime behavior revealed disquieting facets of human nature. One of the places of execution was behind her house in Oviedo, and she could hear the Nationalist firing squads. At that time, she believed that the Republicans were not indulging in wholesale killing, but when she returned to the Republican zone, she was horrified to learn that they had acted in a like manner. *Diario de una maestra (Diary of a Schoolteacher)*, 1961, fictionalizes the novelist's experiences as a teacher and describes the hardships she suffered during the war.

The postwar years brought hunger and great demoralization to Spain. Dolores Medio was particularly impressed by obvious inequities during this time: "When I came to Madrid there were eggs and hams in all the grocery store windows. . . and candy and everything, but we couldn't get them. We had a small ration, a tiny ration of bread as hard as a rock. . . [in a] difficult postwar period, it is necessary to go hungry, but we all should be hungry, even people with money."[5]

II *The Novelist*

A new horizon opened for Miss Medio when she received the Concha Espina Prize in 1945 for her short story "Nina," This decided her in favor of a career in writing, and she moved to Madrid, where she supported herself by tutoring and attended classes in Education and Journalism. For nine years she sublet a room in an apartment shared by other families, an arrangement quite common during the postwar years of housing shortage. She describes the special psychology of the sublessee in many works, notably *Funcionario público (Public Servant)*.

She worked primarily for the newspaper *Domingo* from 1945 until it folded in 1965. At that time she successfully sued the owners for terminating her employment without notification and for other infractions of the work law. After a dramatic trial in which she proved that she had held the position of greatest responsibility on the staff, she won the case and received a small indemnification. According to Miss Medio, the paper was directed toward the least educated of the newspaper-reading public. Twenty years of recasting the news into clear, unadorned prose helped to develop the deliberately simple, straightforward style characteristic of her writing.

She wrote weekly articles for *Domingo* in all fields except politics, sports, and bullfighting. The work enriched her personal experience and increased her knowledge of human nature. She wrote a column for the lovelorn under the name of "Amaranta," which, in her words, she turned into a "laboratory of experimental psychology."[6] The letters she received revealed the true extent of the new materialism: she soon learned that most girls were interested in men with money (in direct opposition to the thesis in her idealistic novel *Selfishness*); that the male correspondents were just as crass. These people, whom she calls the "postwar generation, the hungry generation," afforded her further lessons in human nature, for she was surprised at the lack of idealism in people so young.[7] (She still has thirty thousand note-cards in her possession, each with a separate case study, taken from letters asking "Amaranta" for advice.)

While working for *Domingo,* she continued writing in her spare time, and created the novel which assured her literary success: in 1952 *We Riveros* won the Premio Nadal, one of Spain's most prestigious literary prizes, one which carries with it a sizeable monetary award. From this date on, she has continued to produce fiction at a steady pace. Two short works written in 1954, *Compás de espera (Pause)* and *Mañana (Tomorrow),* revealed Miss Medio's budding interest in the lower classes and their problems. This was confirmed with her second full-length work, *Funcionario público (Public Servant)*, life story of the government white-collar worker in Madrid. Three more novels, two patently autobiographical in character, followed in short succession. *El pez sigue flotando (The Fish Stays Afloat)* in 1959, and *Diario de una maestra (Diary of a Schoolteacher)*, 1961, recreate more of Miss Medio's own experiences in fictional idiom. *Bibiana* (1963) treats the life of the middle-class housewife, again demonstrating Miss Medio's preference for the average over the extraordinary.

In 1962, Miss Medio was wrongly accused of participating in a women's march demanding a pay raise for Asturian mine workers. Although she did not take part in the demonstration, she was in the vicinity and was taken into custody. When the police learned that she was an Asturian, she was fined and then jailed for a month when she could not pay the fine. She later transferred part of this incident to one of her novels, *Bibiana*, and also wrote another work about the women she met in jail which has not been published because of the censorship. She discussed plans for this novel in an interview for a newspaper: "Yes, in *Celda común [Prison Ward]* there appear many lives that were close to me in that month in 1962 that I spent in the Ventas jail. . . . During my stay there I met thieves, prostitutes, murderesses. . . . My novel will be 'life in a women's prison.'"[8]

Since 1966, she has alternated fiction with other types of literature. A short novel and a collection of short stories (*El señor García*, 1966, and *Andrés*, 1967) have been her contributions to fiction; two biographies (*Isabel II de España*, 1966, and *Selma Lagerlöf*, 1971) and a guidebook to Asturias (*Asturias*, 1971) are incursions into the realm of nonfiction.

Many of her stories have been adapted for presentation on Spanish television, and the reedition of several books proves her continuing popularity. Her works have had a modest success outside of Spain: translations into several languages, notably into Russian (Miss Medio is not sure of the count, since most have been pirated editions), as well as the adaptation of some of her fiction for classroom editions, indicate a growing interest in her work.[9]

III *Philosophy and Literary Creation*

Dolores Medio's literary philosophy centers on her concept of the reproduction of reality as the single most important factor in

literature. Literary reality, however, includes more than a simple
transference of observed or experienced data into fictional form.
Miss Medio has explained what she means in an expanded definition
of the word "autobiography":

[. . .] [it] is not only what the author has lived in a real and effective way,
imposed at times by chance, and which may not even have the slightest
connection with his personality, but also something very important:
what the novelist has *not* lived in a material way, but what he *could* have
lived, if circumstances, which are so decisive (or perhaps more imperative
than heredity), had permitted. We cannot deny the importance of this
latent force, which in psychology is called "possibilities of the personality."[10] (The italics are Miss Medio's.)

Literary creation must take a personal reality as artistic raw
material and then refine it into the finished fictional product. The
author thus ardently defends the use of autobiograhical material,
which makes the novel a "[. . .] human document, giving it a sense
of authenticity, of unquestionable precision, which could be lacking
in a purely imaginative work."[11]
There must be, however, an interval which allows the artistic
elaboration of the original event, or the redirection of sensations,
experience, or even data so they may reflect an artistic reality
rather than a merely personal one:

How is the idea born?. . . We know how knowledge is produced, but
not when. All the things which parade before our senses penetrate through
them and are recorded on that tape, on that virgin film which is the brain.
Everything is recorded, but not everything is elaborated, assimilated, in
short converted into idea, but rather it is stored—often without an acknowledged receipt—in the darkroom of the subconscious. Bringing to light those
latent impressions is the task of the psychoanalyst [. . .] of the educator
[. . .] and [. . .] of the novelist.[12]

The logical continuation of the theory of a subjectively created
reality as a basis for fiction is the idea that literature should reflect
life as it is today, life as interpreted by the author. For this reason
her books (with the exception of the first novel) are contemporary
in setting and make use of the data that she herself gathers; the
personal experiences which she blends into the fictional work are
only part of an elaborate system of preparation. For example, she
carefully documented working conditions at the telegraph office
for her novel *Public Servant*.

Words like "document" and "observation" appear time and again in her interpretation of what literature should be. She has always advocated these Realistic techniques as the foundation of the novel: "observation is a very important quality for novelists";[13] "[. . .] each writer would do well to develop himself within the world he knows best, thus giving testimony, with his novels, to what he has seen and verified with his experience. . ."[14]

Her own life style is quite modest: "She travels on the subway or the bus, buys clothing from the large department stores or from ready-made clothing shops, she frequents the markets, movies, cafés, and modest restaurants where she generally finds the characters for her novels."[15] Her identification with the people and atmosphere she describes ties together the two ideas about autobiographical material and the necessity to reflect contemporary life. By writing only about the segment of society with which she is most familiar, she achieves a sense of complete authenticity gained only from first-hand experience.

IV *History, Literary Theory, and Character*

A most effective way to present contemporary life through the novel is to consider literature as another means of writing history. Speaking of the contemporary novel in general, Miss Medio states, "Each one of the novels, without pretensions of writing history, narrates the *pequeño vivir* [everyday life] of characters who move within a certain milieu and a determined period [...] from the study of all these one can deduce the life style of our country during the present times, the Spanish evolution and revolution which we ourselves have lived through, better than it could be studied in a textbook."[16]

If history is not made up of cataclysmic events, but of a compendium of everyday occurrences which typify the life of the period, then characters who reflect this idea must be ordinary people whose lives are completely representative. "In fact, I prefer the 'antihero' [to the 'hero'] because he seems even more heroic to me, precisely because he is unnoticed in a society which is so fond of showy events [. . .] I prefer a man who is not flashy but is effective for the smooth running of society, although his position probably won't be appreciated at the time of the victories."[17] The student of Spanish literature can see in these words an echo of Miguel de Unamuno's theory of "intrahistory,"[18] or, in an even closer source, the same principles in an essay by the philosopher José Ortega y Gasset in *El espectador (The Spectator)*, one of Miss Medio's favorite works.[19]

Miss Medio's preference for the lower or middle classes, her desire to present exterior reality and then penetrate beyond it, show the influence of the idea of intrahistory. The writer must expose specifically contemporary problems: the novel may not distort social reality but, at the very least, should reflect existing conditions. One constant that seems to characterize modern civilization is the dehumanization of man, brought about through too rapid progress and a philosophy oriented toward the common good rather than the individual one, a process which she describes fictionally in the conflict of man with rigid forms of society which do not make sufficient allowance for the individual. Her own analysis of contemporary society and its shifting values is based on the conclusion that certain aspects of Spain's socioeconomic structure are changing too fast for its traditional essence, thus creating an imbalance that she hopes can be remedied by time.[20] At present, economic prosperity is preceding the educational orientation that would teach people how to handle the new affluence. One of her unpublished works, *El diablo no compra almas (The Devil Doesn't Buy Souls)*, refers to the fact that today the Devil no longer has to tempt people, since they practically give him their souls.[21] Another novel, now in press, treats the theme of the nouveau riche and how the sudden acquisition of money affects a family.[22]

V   *The Function of the Novel*

The social realists in contemporary Spanish literature generally fictionalize specific problems in society, pointing to much-needed reforms (occupational, social, ethical). Miss Medio also holds a place in this group; her own analysis of the term "social" means a novel that blends the historical and the social. This is more in the vein of nineteenth-century Realism than in that of the contemporary emphasis on literature as a quasi-documentary depiction of socio-economic conditions.

Miss Medio's interpretation of the constituent elements of the "social novel" is thus seen to be much more comprehensive than the usual definition: the historical novel, for example, is also "social" because it provides the biography of an epoch.[23] Simply by writing about man, the novel will necessarily be social, since it will concern man in relation with his milieu.

Miss Medio disagrees with the theory of art for art's sake, for although the novel does not have to be purposefully sociological, it is, in the long run, part of the educative process, and is therefore "social" in the broadest interpretation of the word. This effect may be negative (in the case of the sensational work, replete with murders, or in the sentimental novel; both of these to a degree evade reality). The mere possibility that the novel may influence the reader, says Miss Medio, puts a definite responsibility on the writer. This does not mean, however, that art must bow before the idea. In a statement reminiscent of some basic tenets of Ortega y Gasset in his essay "Ideas sobre la novela" ("Ideas on the Novel"), she states that the deliberate insertion of a message—whether social, political, or religious—undermines the aesthetic ideal and turns it into propaganda.

Literature, however, must have a higher mission than simple entertainment, and Miss Medio is very much aware of a double duty as writer and teacher: "The untutored reader, and even the average reader, undoubtedly belongs to the category of mass man. And one should not give the mass man, like the child, what he asks for, but rather what is good for him, making him think, of course, that that is what he wants." She continues, "Reading forms part of education, not only of aesthetics, [. . .] but of the total formation of man. Then, in my judgment—now the educator rather than the writer is talking—directing the reading of the masses is an obligation of all of us who are interested in the education of the people."[24]

Her intention of using the novel for instructional purposes is reflected as well in a series of articles entitled "Lo social en la novela" ("Social Material in the Novel"). She shows a strong influence of Ortega y Gasset in these articles and quotes from his "La deshumanización del arte" ("The Dehumanization of Art"), which touches on the relationship of the work of art with reality. She takes the position that social material is anything that elucidates man's place in the world, thus taking a radically different view of the general definition of "social."

She distinguishes between two types of social novel: the novel which contains social material and the novel as an "educative medium fulfilling an undoubtedly social function." She justifies the inclusion of this second type of social novel when she describes

what she considers to be an intimate connection between the social
and the historical novel, joined in the instructional possibilities
they offer. She cites *Uncle Tom's Cabin* and *Gone with the Wind*
as examples of this kind of novel, which describes events important
to the history of a large segment of humanity. By studying the
everyday life of the characters who move within a given environment, one can deduce the way of life in that country. This method
provides new perspectives for the reader.[25] She puts her theory of
"social literature" into practice by describing the relationship
between the average person and the atmosphere in which he lives,
and the cause-and-effect of problems (social and emotional) which
show up in the character and personality of her protagonist. Although she has most thoroughly studied the effects of heredity
and environment in the first novel (and even used these very words
in analyzing her characters), the Naturalist approach to the novel has never been very far from her mind. She continues with
this idea in the aforementioned article in her statement that there
is an intimate relationship between body and soul which also exists
between man and his environment. Man, product of heredity and
environment, cannot be conceived of as outside of the social environment. For this reason any real and human novel must be
social in this sense.[26]

VI *Literary Affinities: Style*

Miss Medio's tastes in literature, although eclectic (she cites
Baroja, Valle-Inclán, and Miró among some of her favorites), run
preferably to the Realists:

> "My favorite authors were always those which we can consider today
> as the [modern] classics, that is, the great authors of the past century and
> of the beginning of our century. Among ours, the Spaniards, Galdós,
> Clarín, Baroja [. . .] In general, I prefer Realistic authors, Spanish as well
> as foreign, although I also read authors of science fiction as well as those
> of Romantic persuasion and those who prefer intellectualized content.
> I read them out of curiosity and because I should be acquainted with them,
> but I prefer the Realists."[27]

The choice is not surprising, considering her procedure of using
observed reality as the basis of her fiction. Another point of contact
is their commonly-shared preference for the middle class as novelistic material.

As for her interest in style, this reflects her concern for the reader and her own pedagogical methods as a teacher: "I suppose that the most important quality of style is clarity [. . .] The modern novel [. . .] endowed with a dynamism which the [modern] classical novel [of Spain] did not need, demands the brevity of a rapid, direct, clean style which doesn't tire the reader."[28] The model to which she turns is most revealing: She chooses the philosopher Ortega y Gasset rather than a novelist, a preference which again recalls the expository techniques of teaching, as she comments on Ortega's method of breaking the complex into simple terms. "I do not believe that there is another writer who handles our language with the austerity and beauty with which Ortega does, and he never uses long paragraphs, the kind that oblige the reader to go back constantly to look for the original idea that engendered the paragraph."[29]

The frame into which Dolores Medio intends to set her novels is now clear. Her main preoccupations, of both a human and social nature, find their way into her works as recurrent themes, often based on her own experience and knowledge of reality. She states that the novelist acts as a medium through which the characters express themselves almost spontaneously: "[The novelist] should simply create a novel, literature. The characters that the novelist sets up will take charge of living their lives [. . .]"[30] Thus, in her literary credo, she must reflect rather than fabricate her material, yet her observations are tempered with a warmth and sympathy toward her fellow man that transcend the position of objective witness to a social reality.

CHAPTER 3

The Early Works: Short Narrative
1945–1954

THE decade 1945–1955 was a decisive one for Dolores Medio. She received two literary prizes and decided to become a professional writer.

Along with the prize-winning novel, *Nosotros los Rivero (We Riveros)*, Miss Medio produced a number of short stories. Her newspaper work doubtlessly affected her choice of form: the special demands of reporting, and the economy of space and words peculiar to newspaper composition made her adept at concision, which she then applied to her short fiction.

I "Nina"

"Nina" won the Concha Espina Prize in 1945,[1] which encouraged Miss Medio to devote herself to full-time writing. The story is written in the *tú* form, the second person singular denoting familiarity with the person addressed. A man has encountered a childhood friend who is now a prostitute working from a low-class bar. He remembers their youth in a small provincial town and the circumstances that led her inevitably to become what she is: she was the daughter of a crone whose name was enough to make the children run away when Nina came into the square. She spent her childhood in poverty, living in a hut in almost animal-like misery. Since the children would not play with her (a precocious manifestation of their cruelty as adults), she found solace at the old fountain in the middle of the square, which the author refers to as "the old grandmother": "The plaza of our town—do you remember it?— was small, intimate, modest, like the patio of a large, shabby manor house. And the fountain . . . The little old fountain which stood in the center of it, was your friend. In the summer afternoon, it would flow slowly, lazily, taking its siesta in the sun. You would sit in its warm lap and play at waking it" (p. 379).

Like birds of prey, the young men of the town wait for Nina to grow up in order to take advantage of her helplessness. She disappears one day, and the town believes that she has been swept away by the river. Thus the narrator, one of the men who could have ruined her, but did not because of the tenderness and compassion that Nina inspired in him, finally discovers her in the basest of situations. Yet despite the clinging dress and heavy makeup, her eyes still retain the purity—and the fear—of childhood.

The serious theme underlying the sentimentality of the story saves "Nina" from the bathos of escape literature. Obviously, the marked difference between Nina and the other children is a social distinction, and a sort of environmental determinism pushes Nina toward the inevitable. Her tragedy here stems from the attitude of others, the causative factor being "what is expected" of a girl in her position. The author's sympathy for Nina is clear in the descriptions of her still childlike eyes, even in her state of degradation.

Comparisons point to man's cruelty and nature's goodness. The sympathetic qualities of nature, its inherent peacefulness, contrast with the nature of man, corrupted and corrupting. Nina is likened to a frightened animal, a flower destroyed by a clumsy foot, or clear water muddied by man quenching his thirst. Her blamelessness is further signaled by references to her fear, her unusual beauty, and her clear eyes. The narrator even defends nature in connection with Nina's supposed death, while pointing to man's essentially destructive tendencies: "Even if [the river] arrives at our village agitated, dirty, and in a bad mood once in a while, it is still noble . . . "(p. 384). Man's inhumanity causes more destruction than nature's forces (the Civil War—not the racing river—demolished the bridge at Peñarán), an analogue to the fact that his cruelty also caused Nina's disappearance.

The flaws of this early piece are sentimentality, a language which relies heavily on elaborate literary devices (metaphors, high-flown similes, rhetorical questions) and exaggerated descriptions. But the defects are offset in great part by Miss Medio's convincing revelation of human motives. The emphasis of the work is not on the end result (the prostitution), but on the reasons *why* Nina should have become a prostitute. Nina, according to the author-narrator, is not at fault here, for she views the girl as a product of society. The human and social content, plus the basic simplicity of the story itself, doubtless showed the jury of the Concha Espina Prize that they had a promising writer in Dolores Medio.

II   Compás de espera (Pause)

Compás de espera (Pause) was the first collection of short stories, published in 1954.[2] Although the intervening novel *We Riveros* showed a markedly different approach from the first short story, Miss Medio returned to the type of narration she used in "Nina," revealing an abiding interest in content drawn from the milieu of the lower class.

The title takes its name from the first story, and the "pause" refers to the period between a cave-in in an Asturian mine and the time when the bodies are brought up. Several lives intersect at this point, brought together by their common tragedy. Leaving the reader in suspense as to the outcome of the cave-in, Miss Medio introduces the circumstances and the relationship of the survivors to the miners: Nora, happy-go-lucky wife of one of them, who convinced her husband to become a miner and leave farming; Juancho, who had survived another cave-in and is not surprised that the mine should take his only son in revenge for losing him; the orphaned Muntaner brothers who learn that the youngest is now under the ground; Marta, abused and neglected by her husband, has turned her hopes and affections to her oldest boy, Rufo, who is also trapped.

After the bodies are brought out, Miss Medio catalogues the reactions of each family: the hysterics of the young wife, the stoical acceptance with no show of emotion on the part of the men; the madness of Marta.

With a strong sense for dramatic contrast, Dolores Medio suggests that we have become indifferent to the sacrifices and tragedies of others, especially when they are of the lower classes. She reduces the event to cold statistics: "That was all. All, that is, for the press, for the world, which fixes its indifferent eyes on small tragedies" (p. 5). Compared to the Korean War, or a coronation, this event is insignificant: "One understands that such a common, ordinary event, which happened there in the mines of Asturias, would not take up more than a small space"(p. 5). At the end of the story a train loaded with coal goes by, and Juancho shakes his fist at it, shouting, "And they say coal is expensive." The comparison of what is costly to the consumer and to the miner reveals the dreadful change of perspective. By the irony of these words the author tries to impress the reader with her "thesis": the human element must take precedence over any other consideration. The fact that these people are of a lower class does not make their unhappiness any less tragic. The mine is personified as a threat to the workers, a monster that exacts tribute, or wild beast which devours human flesh. The device emphasizes the helplessness of the workers and the dangers inherent in their profession.

By playing with several intersecting stories, dividing them into reaction to the disaster and final realization of the inevitable, Miss Medio has created a maximum of tension in a short space of time. The balanced combination of the social with human content—with neither outweighing the other—will be a constant in later works.

The division between classes, and the general lack of concern toward those who serve us most faithfully is further developed in "El cuadro" ("The Picture"). The author sees a portrait of a woman in the office of an internationally known doctor; although the subject does not seem to be anyone famous, there is a bouquet of roses below the painting, as if in homage. The doctor readily complies when asked the history of the picture: The woman was Ana-Antonia, who in effect sacrificed her youth to bring up the doctor when he lost his mother at an early age. Too late he realized his ingratitude in taking this altruism for granted; the flowers under the portrait now pay homage to Ana-Antonia after her death. This is the clearest concession to date of the emotional distance that separates the classes; the economic factor may be inevitable in this society, but human understanding must cross barriers to establish communication and sympathy. The doctor voices Miss Medio's opinions:

> The story of Ana-Antonia is a common one. The girl who gave her young master her dreams of youth as a present is a common woman. Everything is common. Nothing is of great consequence. Her dreams—hardly anything. Bah! What are dreams worth, what is the life of a small-town girl worth? . . . The general who wins a spectacular battle is applauded . . . and the learned man who at last hunts down unknown bacteria in his microscope. . . . And the artist who beautifies our life with his works. But no one salutes with emotion that legion of women, those girls whose story is too common to interest us, those who work and suffer in anonymity, making possible the triumph of those who reach their goal. And Ana-Antonia was simply that: a common girl." (p. 38)

In "El hombre del violín" ("The Man with the Violin"), a woman waiting for a train spies a violin on the platform and imagines what the owner is like and what a pleasant travelling companion he would make. A romantic-looking youth fits her idea, and she conjures up a whole history to fit his appearance. When a shabbily-dressed man picks up the case and climbs onto the train, she accuses him of trying to steal the boy's instrument, and is terribly embarrassed to learn that he is really the owner. This case of mistaken identity is an indictment of the way we categorize others only through their appearance. The woman's words prove this point: "That man. . . . That man who *looks like a beggar* has stolen your violin" (p. 50, emphasis added). The ragged man had a right to his violin, yet the woman took it for granted that since he was not dressed for the part of an artist he must be a thief.

"Delito impune" ("Unpunished Crime") is the last story in the collection and draws the greatest sympathy in that combination of sentimental emphasis on unhappiness or poverty made hopeless by class distinctions. Juana Marín sits on a park bench thinking about her desperate situation. Except for her little girl, she is alone in the world, with no money and almost no prospects for a job. A rich child runs up and Juana plays with her until her nurse indignantly whisks her away. Only then does she see that the child has forgotten an expensive doll. Torn between taking it and returning it, Juana finally decides to bring it home to her child, who has never had an expensive toy. The reader follows her thoughts and self-accusations, for she knows full well the "magnitude" of her crime. The child's joy contrasts with Juana's guilt as she hugs the child and cries.

The note of pathos is the dominant emotion in the book. There seems to be no happiness possible for this class of people; not only do they have their own misery to contend with, but they are confronted with the ease and happiness of the upper-class level as well as the ingratitude of the people they serve. The stress on poverty and the sacrifice that must accompany it is another dominant note which will continue in later works.[3] Although several of these stories sin on the side of exaggerated emotional content, this collection has elements which the author more successfully integrates into later works, where understatement rather than melodrama will be the rule. Nevertheless, *Pause* has an impact that belies its tiny size (the book measures 3 x 4 inches), for the misery of the protagonists, trapped without hope of escape, strikes an empathic chord with the reader.

III Mañana (Tomorrow)

The novelette *Mañana (Tomorrow)* also appeared in this period.[4] The reader can easily recognize some of the concerns already developed in Miss Medio's previous short works, although in place of the specific social content (the need for reform), she comments on man's freedom of action.

Jenara is a young woman whose dull and pathetic existence up to this point has been determined by others. When her father died, she was placed in an orphanage, where her mother for a time visited her infrequently, then not at all. The impersonal treatment she received there ended her happy childhood: " . . . Jenara was inmate number fifty-three. Or number twenty-five. Or seventeen. She got to be number two. But always that: a number. A number and a name pronounced distractedly, when they were in class, or had to answer questions. Nara, little Nara [Jenara's nickname] had died at the same time as her father, whom she no longer remembered" (p. 10). The dehumanization Jenara noticed as a child became even more obvious when she made her way in the world: In her monotonous job as ticketseller in the subway her movements are automatic, her vocabulary limited to directions, and the buyers come and go so fast that she cannot get to know them as people. Her rented room and lack of family complete the uneventful, cheerless pattern of her life. Nara fights against the impersonalization of her existence with a game in which she identifies the livelihood and personality of the ticketbuyers by their hands, thus adding a dramatic facet to their lives and, by extension, to hers.

Nara finally decides that she must make an effort to change the monotony of her life, and thus accepts a position as nurse-companion to a sick child in Galicia. She takes the train there, and it is on this trip that the reader learns of Nara's plans for the future mixed with her remembrances of the past. By coincidence, she meets a student who is related to the people for whom she will work, and he paints a glowing picture of life there, describing the warm family relationship and sweet child in attractive terms. There is no doubt that this change is for the best, and Nara is quite excited about her new prospects.

The true significance of this change is in the nature of the choice: Nara is the only one responsible for this decision. Her words evoke the existential tenet of self-determination through free resolution:

Why do they speak of the destiny of people? Was I destined to be a ticket agent? What nonsense. No one is destined to anything. The solution to our problems is always in our hands. Our acts are the only ones which count. I have always said it. We are products of our actions. Right now, if I hadn't decided to take this step I would be at the ticket window. Like yesterday, like last month, like ten years ago. Then? It is I, only I who decides, who has her destiny in her own hands. I can't stand people who complain about their luck, without doing anything to change it. Do they live well? Do they live poorly? They live the way they want. That's it. The way they want. (pp. 34–35)

A derailment causes an unexpected stop, and as the train is to be delayed by several hours, the passengers are allowed to get off and walk to the nearby station. There Nara meets a man who buys her coffee and offers to go for a walk with her. Ignoring the hurt look on the student's face, she accepts, and the two decide to explore the countryside. She feels attracted to this mysterious stranger, whom she feels she has known all her life, and thus it is natural for her to give herself to him freely, without ties. When it is time to go, they arrive at the station only a minute before the train is to leave, and he offers her the choice of staying with him or continuing with her plans. With only seconds left, she decides to remain, and rushes onto the train to pick up her suitcase, which falls open, spilling its contents. As she hurriedly tries to stuff the clothing back in, the train begins to move and she cannot get off. She realizes that she doesn't even know the man's name; his voice is lost in the wind as the train picks up speed:

But her voice, and his, were lost in the night, between the noises of the two trains, which, like their lives, were separating after hardly having made contact. Nara continued shouting. Her shout was a howl. All the anguish of the absurd and unexpected situation escaped from her in that call, which remained unanswered: "Your name! . . . Your name!" (p. 64)

Nara's idea of life has proved to be completely mistaken. Her decision was overruled by "circumstance," the very concept she had denied so vigorously. Yet coincidence has ruled her life since she left Madrid. Without the accidental train stop, she never would have met the man; her decision to abandon her plans was reversed by the train's departure. The step she has taken in order to fulfill her own life through that of another—the answer to her desire to be a human being instead of a number, a worker, a nursemaid—has ironically been blocked by a series of circumstances which we would call fate, chance, or destiny. The title, which refers to the new life she has chosen for herself, takes on an ironic note, since the new job will now be colored by the memory of what could have been. The use of alternating present and past, filtered through the screen of Nara's memories, enhances the content. The time factor is another dimension of the idea of choice, destiny, and circumstance. The past has determined her outlook in the present; the future offers the unknown factor in multiple "possibilities": a new life in Galicia, a new life with the stranger. In addition, the effective use of the time element within Nara's "present" creates a skillful blend of suspense and anticipation for the reader (i.e., will she miss the train, will she get off the train?).

In *Tomorrow*, as in earlier collections, Miss Medio presents a person of the lower classes who is a victim of indifference on various levels. In this story, the indifference is the refusal of others to separate her from the anonymous mass of people like her, and the final impossibility of attaining individuality even after an effort. The author's sympathy is clearly with the protagonists, who, contrary to their opinions, are simply victims of their environment or circumstances which control their lives. By using a person who is not distinguished in any way, the author presents another "ordinary life" which has been denied the opportunity to fulfill itself. The emphasis, however, is not on class oppression, but on the emotional impact of specifically human reactions to a given set of circumstances.

The simple plot line of the story, the directness with which Miss Medio presents the situation, the simplicity of the language and emphasis on inner thought and human problems with a minimum of author intervention (either through the medium of style or direct commentary) present the story from a different perspective compared to the more traditional descriptive techniques of *We Riveros*. The concision and rapidity of presentation, the economy of descriptive details, the emphasis on emotional reaction are all improvements over the other short works. The story is well done and is perhaps the best of the early works.

IV   *"Patio de luces" ("The Courtyard")*

"Patio de luces" ("The Courtyard"), a short story which appeared in 1954,[5] describes the unspoken love of a timid shopkeeper for a mysterious woman who sells needlework on commission in his store. This piece, expanded and changed somewhat, was incorporated into a later novel, *El pez sigue flotando (The Fish Stays Afloat)* and will be discussed in that chapter.

Although the works composed during this period vary greatly in subject matter, a common philosophy and similar technical devices offer an interesting unity. The characters are all from the lower classes, with no extraordinary qualities. In general, their lives take some decisive turn which is caused by a chance occurrence rather than a self-made decision. Invariably, they become victims of the situation: if they challenge life, they lose; attempts to better themselves end in failure.

The relationship among the characters reveals an even unhappier situation. Although Miss Medio emphasizes common problems (the mining disaster, lack of money, loneliness), the solidarity which could have provided the most elementary basis of communication is missing; each is confined to the narrow circle of his own troubles and cannot (or will not) step out to help the other. A more active contempt for or indifference to others is apparent: The gap that separates the classes is too wide to allow crossing; preconceived ideas about others hinder accepting the man instead of his appearance.

The pathos of the situation, the helplessness of the individual in the face of something beyond his control (be it destiny or the social structure) is rendered the more poignant through the use of strong contrasts (in plot as well as literary devices) designed to elicit maximum sympathetic response on the part of the reader.

CHAPTER 4

The First Novel

W E *Riveros* gave an auspicious start to Dolores Medio's career as a novelist: this first novel won her the prestigious Premio Eugenio Nadal 1952.[1] The award gave immediate rise to a polemic which seriously questioned Miss Medio's right to receive the prize. Perhaps the detractors expected something startlingly innovational that year; if that was the case, they had reason to be disappointed, for this novel is related to narrative forms of the preceding century and the traditional realism of Spain's nineteenth-century literary masters. The story unfolds in linear disposition with no experimentation in time, language, or form. Although written in the third person, it is an autobiographical work in a double sense, since the heroine remembering her past is actually the alter ego of the novelist who is recreating her life, and many of the characters are modeled after people in her life.[2]

II   Nosotros los Rivero—We Riveros

The arrival of the main character, Lena Rivero, on the train, marks her return to the Oviedo she left as a young woman. Personal reminiscence mingles with historical constants as she explores her city again, noting the changes with bittersweet nostalgia. Lena finally gives herself over completely to memory, thus introducing "We Riveros"—the Rivero family—: her father "El Aguilucho" ("The Eaglet"), who died when she was nine, her domineering mother, often insensitive to the needs of her children, Aunt Mag, her beautiful half-sister Heidi, who runs away early in the novel, and her sister María and brother Ger. The main story opens in the days following Mr. Rivero's death; young Lena's sense of loss is especially keen, since her greatest ties were with her father, who seemed to understand her in a way her mother could not and never would. The reality of death strikes her as she sees mourning clothes being made, and the empty places where her beloved father used to sit. The tragedy also brings up another unpleasant memory: the legend of the curse of the Riveros: a "terrible inheritance" (p. 19) which weighs on a family in which no one dies in bed. The reader learns of the mystery as a family friend tells the background of the curse: during the amortization of church property, no one dared to buy a certain piece of land which belonged to the friars. Since the land produced excellent fruit, a Rivero finally purchased it, scoffing at the curse which was now supposed to be attached to it. He died soon after, however, and generation after generation of Riveros suffered accidental deaths. As for the women of the family: "in short, ladies, it's best not to speak of them" (p. 40).

Although the author does not linger too long on the immediate effects of the father's death, the memory and influence of this man permeate the first part of the novel. Although he never appears as a character in his own right, the reminiscences of Lena and the others create a special aura of grandeur around him:

> His natural restlessness led him to be a proprietor of a sugar plantation . . . , a rancher on the shores of the Plata River, a rubber worker in the Amazon jungles which were hardly explored, a planter in Florida, a banker in New York . . . he was a volunteer . . . in the war with Cuba, but in battles of love . . . Germán Rivero was always a perfect international soldier. And of course, a magnificent type of adventurer, with all the characteristics of men of this kind: valiant, a dreamer, arrogant. . . . He searched laboriously for gold and squandered it when he had it . . ." (pp. 53–54)

He is also stoic in the face of extreme bad luck (he shrugs his shoulders at the failure of a bank where he kept his hard-earned money, and later when his prosperous shop burns down).

"The Eaglet" is a symbol of the Rivero family, the cohesive force which holds them together. With his death, the dissolution begins, slow and unobserved at first, as each of the characters begins to assert his personality and pulls away. The children's individual traits start to form, and the family naturally comes into conflict:

> The death of "The Eaglet" had broken the chain which linked the family necklace. Because the Riveros were like a necklace of colored beads, linked by the weak red string of blood. The same and different. Impossible for them to remain united once the silk was broken. (p. 70)

The story soon splits into three different but mutually dependent parts: first, Lena's adventures, reactions, and her transition from adolescence to womanhood; second, but still important, the lives of the other Riveros, both in their contact with Lena and in their own right; and third, the story of an entire epoch, interpreted in micro-cosmic form through the events that take place in Oviedo and through the impact that history has on this family. The novelist controls these three threads with such skill that none—with the possible exception of Lena's more dramatic problems—takes exclusive hold over the narration, and that each directly bears on the other, so that it would be difficult to untangle the cause and effect.

The father's death signals a spiritual break in the heretofore smooth life of the Riveros; soon after, their existence also changes materially. They have to give up the store and their house, which have been condemned. The new economic situation caused by the loss of their income and the necessity of finding new lodgings begins the first of a series of steps marking a decline in the family's fortunes: the new house is sad looking and too large (p. 140); their friends quickly desert them; they must learn to economize in all aspects of their daily lives, and finally must pawn the family possessions in order to live. These new circumstances bring out the personalities of the family. The first dramatic change is the cat, Kedi-Bey, who symbolizes the fate of the entire family. He dies soon after the move because, according to the children, he is unable to adjust. He is an *inadaptado*, a favorite word of the author's and a term which could as easily apply to Mrs. Rivero, who could never reconcile herself to her situation.

After the move, the author concentrates on Lena, who is becoming a young lady. Her youthful independence has not been curbed; she continues to chafe at her mother's ideas of the proper behavior for a woman. Not the least of the sources of friction are Lena's forbidden excursions into the country to escape the reality of the present and her mother's harsh demands. In these episodes the reader can easily sense the conflict which maturity has created in Lena; the woman she is becoming realizes that there are responsibilities to accept, and a role to assume in the family as well as society. However, there still remains the spirit of the child she was— mischievous but honest with herself and others. Lena's childlike attributes encourage her to go into the country, a symbolic evasion of the hypocrisy of adulthood. Her mother refuses to understand this need and assiduously tries to educate Lena to her "adult" obligations.

Lena's experiences serve double duty in this novel: The main purpose is the revelation of new facets of her character, but they also coincide with the historical perspective, a second major theme of the book. Lena's attitude toward work, for example, reveals her original bent. She doesn't mind labor as long as there is some purpose to it, but the thought of useless, mechanical exertion typified by the thousands of tax receipts she must fill out, bothers her. She later channels some of her energy into making toys, an occupation which allows her to use her creative talents. Work thus opens a new side of life to her. She compares machine-made goods with an artisan's work and realizes why the latter should have some pride: "Modern life demanded, above all, the economy of effort and time, but she lives on the margin of all realities, and that undisciplined work, that artist's work, into which she put her soul, held an enchantment that no [amount of] reason could take from her" (p. 189). This discovery complements the events occurring outside the Riveros' personal story: the struggle of the old and the new appears again, expanded now to include work methods. The nostalgia for the individual's worth, exemplified by hand-made artifacts, also condemns the depersonalization of the machine age.

A different kind of episode introduces a new, more intimate facet of Lena's life, marking symbolically her initiation into adulthood through the introduction to sex by an unscrupulous family friend. The author conveys her antipathy toward this character in an introductory description: as Jauregui approaches Lena, whom he is to meet in the Cathedral, "one would say that he glided rather than walked" (p. 198). Conforming to the traditional concept of the snake, Jauregui is treacherous, capitalizing on his respectable position to take advantage of the girl; and like the snake in Paradise, he offers secret knowledge which suddenly crystallizes Lena's attitude toward men. Such snake imagery holds double significance, for he then reveals secrets of sex to Lena as he tries to seduce her with kisses and pornographic pictures. She swears that she will never marry, and minutes later, alone and frightened, dedicates her life to Christ when she sees an ecce homo in the Cathedral (her "short-lived streak of mysticism," pp. 209–11).

As Lena leaves the Cathedral, she finds people dancing in the streets at the proclamation of the Second Republic. Lena's other horizons expand with her awareness of the political and historical events in Spain at that time. Ger, the symbol of progress, introduces Lena into two new worlds: the intellectual (symbolized by the Ateneo, a literary group), and the political (represented by the Workmen's Center). Lena is still evolving her own personality, so both her house and the Center, which she frequents, reveal antagonistic forces. Lena can fit into neither extreme, and both consider her a misfit: "For the Quintanas, for their friends, for the old acquaintances of the family, Lena was the revolutionary, the girl with common tastes and plebeian sentiments, who made fun of . . . whatever represented tradition and elegance. For the others, for her new friends, for her comrades, she was the *señorita*, the reactionary [. . .]" (p. 267).

Except for Ger and Lena, the rest of the family progressively turn their backs on the events of the year, for different reasons: Mrs. Rivero is sick, Aunt Mag never reads anything but the society page in the newspaper, and María is too busy with her religious preoccupations to pay attention to things of this world.

On October 5, 1934, the revolutionary forces occupy Oviedo, Ger decides his place is with them, and a while later, the mother dies. As usual, the attitudes of the sisters are completely divergent. When facing the possibility of their mother's death, María insists on telling the truth, so she can save her soul; Lena, thinking of life, wants to keep her mother happy by concealing the inevitable. Just before she dies, Mrs. Rivero hears a shell explode and screams out the name of her son, thus dramatically foreshadowing his death, for he is never found. The reaction of the household to Mrs. Rivero's death is rather understated: Aunt Mag takes refuge in her endless string of proverbs; Lena, who does not seem profoundly affected by the loss, thinks of her freedom; María, dignified and reserved, thinks of heaven (p. 302).

At this time a group of young revolutionaries comes in to search the house, and one of them sees María praying for her mother at her makeshift altar. Although these men are notoriously anti-religious, this young miner reveals his alliance to a more humane brotherhood: instead of arresting María, he takes off his hat and sympathizes—he too had a mother who died. The revolutionaries in this novel are depicted as honest, compassionate men.

After the government troops take over, Lena walks around the city, inspecting the ruins and burned buildings. The University, partially destroyed by fire, is the symbol of her own youth; a change in vocabulary acknowledges the significance of this destruction and the end of an era, emphasizing Lena's new maturity by switching from the youthful nickname Lena to the more appropriate Magdalena. She looks at the charred ruins which represented her childhood:

There her mischievous childhood was buried. And there was the best of
Ger's youth. There were the young yearnings of so many generations of
students [. . .] But all that, what could it matter to her [. . .] She must
not be displeased. She must not shout! [. . .] Raising her tensed fists defi-
antly at an invisible enemy, she turned to all sides, asking bitterly, "Why have
you done this? Why? Why?" . . . (p. 323)

This reaction and Lena's words are almost the literal transcription
of the author's recollection of her own feelings after the revolution.
Greatly disillusioned with the violent reaction of the people, typified
by the burning of the University and the glorious future for which
it stood, young Dolores also felt the bitter disappointment of an un-
fulfilled dream.[3]

Other changes in attitude disclose Lena's new status. She thinks
of the young miner who came to the house, and identifies
him with her former idol, the Prince of Asturias. This radical switch
in class preference reveals a new maturity. She is now obviously
accepting the new order instead of the old, which has shown itself
to be invalid; she symbolically abandons the fantasies of childhood
for a more concrete reality (since his visit to Oviedo, the Prince
of Asturias had been the object of young Lena's daydreams).
Royalty can be the subject of reveries, but obviously not of real life.
Thus the revolution has marked and changed everyone's life:
Lena has been freed—of family and of the past—and intends to leave
for Madrid to become a writer. María decides to become a mission-
ary (she later dies in Manila), and Ger is presumed dead.

The last chapter returns the reader to the reality of the present
introduced in chapter 1 and the parenthetical reminiscences come
to a close. Lena is now successful, but some of the mischievous
girl still peeps from behind the elegant exterior, as she swings on the
University chains, just as she did when she was little.

II   *Critical Reactions to* We Riveros

Critical judgments concerning *We Riveros* varied, to say the
least, and the flame was fanned because of the Nadal Prize. Oddly
enough, much of the unfavorable propaganda was spread before
the novel even appeared, creating a very inauspicious atmosphere
for its reception.[4] On one hand, critics viciously attacked the novel.
Excerpts from some of these vitriolic judgments show the emotional

tone they took: "not worth while reviewing had it not won the Nadal"; "escape literature"; "the tenderness seems rather to be sweetness"; "forced elegance and elevation of tone which degenerate frequently into sheer vulgarity"; "mediocre adaptation of a North American novel of the kind that bored [. . .] spinsters write"; "pretentious"; "artificial"; "padded"; "amorphous and sluggish."[5] A band of defenders also entered the polemic, justifying the winning of a coveted prize with a noninnovational work. The critic Enrique Sordo is representative of this group; he described the book as "the ethopoeia of the Spanish middle class."[6] Attacks, however, continued for quite a while and often descended to a nonliterary level, alluding to the fact that she was only an elementary school teacher or referring to her personal appearance.[7]

One writer sums up the reactions in the following way: "When this [novel] appeared, there fell upon it a kind of critical avalanche, and not exactly solely from the professional critics. About no other novel published is Spain in these last years have there been said more ferocious things than about *We Riveros*, but it is also true that many eulogistic and understanding articles were written [. . .] Now, all this cannot be the key to the fact that *We Riveros* has become one of the most constant 'best sellers' of the Spanish novel [. . .]"[8]

In spite of adversely critical reactions, the popularity of the novel gained momentum, and the work quickly became a success which has not seemed to diminish with the years. At this time *We Riveros* has gone through eight printings. Its appeal may lie in the fact that Miss Medio is deliberately nonintellectual in her approach to literature, that the human element and the reactions of the ordinary person interest her more than an exploration of the dark recesses of the mind, an analysis of outstanding or abnormal behavior, or the study of a hero. She thus emphasizes the human side of the average person in the novel, and as such appeals to a much wider range of people. In an interview, she stated that she writes deliberately within the reach of everyone,[9] a clear indication that she intends her audience range to be extensive. Her training as a teacher must also have heavily influenced the kind of style which would make her accessible to the majority of the reading public: the breaking of the complex into simple terms, the use of comparisons for explanatory purposes (the society-train simile on pp. 50–51 is an excellent example of this), and the tolerant way in which she accepts human foibles, point to her interest in making her thoughts and feelings immediately apparent to the reader, and especially her compassion for and interest in all human beings.

Even though an undemanding reading public may have accepted the work on its own terms and without critical acumen, the Nadal Prize jury, all critics of wide repute, obviously felt that the novel could stand on its own merits. Perhaps its selection that year was due to a common chord which the story struck in each of the readers, although with varying levels of complexity: the nostalgia for a bygone era, reinforced with a structural device (the technique of the nineteenth-century novel) which is the perfect means of emphasizing the "message."

III   *Technique and Literary Creation*

The censurers of *We Riveros* united in their disapproval of the failure to meet the "exigencies of the present-day novel, and [they agreed that] it would fit better into the norms of the past century."[10] Critics who were disturbed because of this supposed unacquaintance with the latest literary fashions failed to realize that this "old-fashioned" technique was a preferred means of reinforcing the intention of the work. Miss Medio describes a moment of social and political upheaval which has since modified the existence of every Spaniard, and carries with it the great problem of adjustment to the inevitable tension between old and new values. She employs a literary form designed to emphasize the distance between the past and the changes which were responsible for eradicating the last traces of a more traditional way of life.

The technique which Dolores Medio uses in *We Riveros* allies her closely with the Realists and Naturalists of the preceding generations. There is a deliberate avoidance of innovational forms; even the introduction of the social structure as an integral part of the novel does not imply the primarily reformative attitudes of the twentieth century, but places the emphasis on the formative influence of milieu, a concept popular during the Naturalist period. The authors who seem to have most influenced her are the two giants of the nineteenth-century Spanish novel, Benito Pérez Galdós and Leopoldo Alas (Clarín). Similarities in presentation and her own statement as to her preferences in reading material leave little room for doubt that her inspiration and models came from this period.[11] Her presentation and extensive development of a specific time period in Oviedo recall Galdós and his technique of weaving historico-geographical data into his novels to create a total sense of reality.[12] This combination of fiction and history is, in Dolores Medio's case, combined with a wealth of autobiographical material and personal experience in the work. Shared with Galdós, too, is the preference for the same type of characters and a similar class: Novels like *Miau* (*Meow*) or *Misericordia* (*Charity*) study cases of middle-class families who have fallen on hard times, yet cannot accept the reality of the situation, blindly insisting on keeping up appearances. A social code by which they must abide determines their existence, even though it is economically impossible to follow it. A similar approach to this kind of problem is found in Mrs. Rivero's case.

The novelist's statement concerning her reasons for using the middle class almost exclusively for novelistic material links her closely with the nineteenth century in its literary preference for the same class:

I prefer to look for my characters from among the middle class for various reasons: the first, because it is the atmosphere in which I move and naturally the one I know best. . . . I have found that the most memorable novels, those which have created unforgettable characters, were those which have taken the long-suffering and marvelous middle class, bearer of so many human values, as protagonists of the work. It is the class which has the most problems: economic ones and especially ones of a moral nature because of its ambiguous situation, between the other two classes, because of its unstable balance in the economy and its forced "pretense of well-being." Oh, our noble and poor hidalgos! How much greatness and misery there is in their lives. . . . If you know reality and literature, don't be surprised that I look for my characters among the long-suffering middle class, which is an inexhaustible source.[13]

The shifting social structures of this period also prompted Galdós to chronicle the changing status of the middle class.

There have been allusions to *We Riveros* as greatly influenced by "a North American novel,"[14] an apparent reference to *Gone with the Wind*. The specifics of this allegation are wrong, but the general idea is correct: both works describe the end of an era after a traumatic upheaval which was the consequence of or prelude to a civil war. To understand why Miss Medio turns to an old form to express her philosophy, it is necessary to investigate her attitude toward Oviedo itself. Her sincere affection for the city is so felt throughout the book through the protagonist and through literary techniques. Her role as the omniscient author is colored by an extremely subjective approach : the undisguised affection which she shows toward the city and its collective inhabitants parallels the human warmth and understanding which she lavishes on the individual characters. One example of this obvious partiality toward the city will suffice :

> A revolution and a civil war, ripping her [Oviedo's] flesh, covering her epidermis with scars, obliging her to restore her amputated limbs, have changed her appearance slightly, but they have not succeeded in transforming the intimate essence of her being. After suffering the tragic devastation of the war, like a boy when he leaves his bed after a serious illness, Oviedo "gave a stretch" [. . . .] In spite of this thirst for expansion, the sedentary spirit of the population continues pulsating, rebellious, in the streets and plazas of old Oviedo, in her beautiful and romantic corners, like petrified dreams of the past, among the very centenarian stones, covered with mold by the dampness. That goblin of old cities, which scoffs at progress, urbanization [. . .] because it has its peaceful dwelling in the narrow and silent streets of immortal Vetusta, in the shadow of the venerable walls of its Cathedral. There is the soul of Oviedo. A soul composed of grandeur and small miseries, of heroism, of timidities, of renunciations." (p. 10)

The author's affection for Oviedo appears most clearly in the technique of personification, a touch which endows the city with a definite personality, and often raises it to the level of a protagonist.

Furthermore, the constant interplay between tradition and progress, the past and the present, is made manifest throughout *We Riveros*, with regular material and ideological symbols of tradition and progress. One example is the protagonist's search for herself in her youth, seen through complementary descriptions of old Oviedo, accompanied by the everpresent knowledge that the past is being supplanted by modernization (the catalogue of additions to and changes in the city).

Further descriptions of the city evoke the theme of contrast : the past versus the present, tradition opposed to progress, enhances the Rivero family struggle and suggests the idea of the passage of time through continual change. Thus time passing for the individual (punctuated by the deaths and final dissolution of the family) is encompassed by an overwhelming sense of time in the city which is measured in terms of centuries. Although Miss Medio's preference for a more vital outlook is obvious from her characters, her treatment of Oviedo discloses a nostalgia for things past: traditions molded by age seem to have much more personality, while newer sections have not yet acquired the necessary patina. Comparing two parts of town, she says, "(The great artery of the city was a young street, almost newborn. Without personality)" (p. 48).

Decidedly, the new and modern street had snatched the scepter of supremacy and elegance from the old and tired Cimadevilla, which extended its tentacles [. . .] over the old part of the city [. . .]. Since then, Cimadevilla began to sink into the pleasant drowsiness of old streets, which long for the frilliness of starched petticoats and the majestic stiffness of crinolines [. . .]. (pp. 49–50)

Even more noteworthy is the influence of Clarín, whose tutelage Miss Medio has openly acknowledged. She mentions him in *We Riveros*: "[The works of] Pérez de Ayala [another influential author from Oviedo] and 'Clarín' were at that time great 'friends' of Lena and helped her to discover old Oviedo" (p. 175). Some of the harshest criticism of *We Riveros*, however, was directed toward the connection of the work with *La Regenta* (*The Judge's Wife*) by Clarín. There were snide comments and veiled hints of plagiarism, revealing a major misinterpretation of the purpose and technique of the book, which, in a general sense, is deliberately modeled after *The Judge's Wife*. Anyone who writes a work about Oviedo must come to terms with this great novel (a landmark in Spanish literature) for it has made the city the archetypal provincial town. Dolores Medio has accepted Clarín's novel as a challenge, and has cleverly incorporated elements from it instead of continually trying to avoid the similarities.

By reforming elements deliberately taken from *The Judge's Wife*, Dolores Medio has created a modern-day version, using the middle instead of the upper class. This technique presupposes the reader's ability to recollect episodes without the necessity of open acknowledgment, thus reinforcing the atmosphere of nostalgia for things past through technique and references to the nineteenth century.

In broad outline, the two volumes of Clarín's work describe the life of Ana Ozores (often called the Spanish Madame Bovary), the wife of a much older man, who sublimates her frustration and dissatisfaction first through a mystical interpretation of religion (symbolized by the powerful and charismatic priest Fermín de Pas, who is in love with her, although she does not realize this) and later through the flesh (symbolized by don Alvaro Mesía, who tries to seduce her). Spurred on by boredom and a set of circumstances designed to facilitate the seduction, she finally gives in, causing her husband's death, her social ostracism, and the collapse of her secure world. Around the central plot is a myriad of complementary stories, revealing multiple facets of the same problems.

For this reason Miss Medio turns to *The Judge's Wife* as the work which would best evoke the end of an era in Oviedo. To reinforce this retrospective glance, she provides a description of the gatherings at the Rivero house: "In Mrs. Rivero's small living room one lived a century behind the times. Life seemed to have backed up around some of the characters, *who had every appearance of protagonists of a novel from the eighteen-hundreds*: Mrs. Rivero, corseted, sad, stuffed in her smock of blue velvet, faded, like an old print" (p. 257, emphasis added). The reference to the picture also adds to the static quality of the scene. Miss Medio has tried to capture just this feeling for all of Oviedo, at a moment when an inexorable revolution (the end of the Second Republic, the beginning of large-scale industrialization) was to change the entire face of Spain.

The first striking similarity is found in the epigraph of *We Riveros*: "To Immortal Vetusta with my sincere devotion." Vetusta was Clarín's code name for Oviedo, and would orient any literate reader toward an immediate association of the novels through the common name. He would not have to go very far to see the next parallel. Both novels have the same opening line. Clarín begins his with the ironic words, "The heroic city of Vetusta was taking a nap"; Miss Medio states, "Oviedo is a sleeping city" (p. 9). Further, both continue with a panoramic description of the city.

Although the plot lines do not bear direct parallels, certain ideas and episodes do. Fermín de Pas and Alvaro Mesía represent opposing ideologies, tradition (the Church) versus innovation (atheism and materialism). Ana Ozores is torn between them, gives herself finally to don Alvaro, and her world is destroyed. In a like manner, but with different action, Lena Rivero is presented with the choice between the old and the new; her world of tradition ends with the Revolution and destruction of the old order. Ana goes through a period of mysticism; so does Lena. Each household has a crafty servant whose first loyalty is to himself and who tries to profit by the situation (Ana's Petra; Rivero's Cheni). The Cathedral is a focal point in both their lives, the material sign of stability, yet in it events take place for both protagonists which symbolize the change in their lives : both are kissed there by characters who are described in repulsive terms (Jauregui and the snake imagery; the acolyte likened to a toad.).

In more general terms, both weave a dense background fabric of people and incidents to reinforce the import of the work; minor characters bring out and elucidate major aspects of the main characters. Oviedo is a protagonist in its own right, with detailed descriptions of its physical characteristics, special atmosphere, and mentality of the citizens which affect the protagonists. Unlike Clarín, however, Dolores shows her affection for "Vetusta" and avoids the biting irony of the earlier work.

Clarín and Miss Medio show affinities in style and technique as well. Each uses psychological study to enhance character development. Of even greater significance is Clarín's connection with the late Realistic-Naturalistic movements, and certain of these techniques also place Miss Medio within the framework of the same trend. The influence of environment on character, and the emphasis on hereditary tendencies are carefully developed throughout the work, beginning with the reason for Lena's return to Oviedo ·

Lena Rivero defended, in her articles and in her novels, the influence of hereditary factors over environment, as a determining factor of the personality. She believed she had reason to do so. The Riveros knew something about heredity by experience. It was environment that Magdalena was looking for then. She wanted to feel it again. She wanted to merge into it, in a somewhat unconscious desire of finding another justification for her absurd youth in the setting of her rebellious childhood. (p. 11)

Later in the work, the author uses two favorite characters—the Ger-Lena duo—as her spokesmen in a discussion about the effects of heredity and environment on the individual: According to Ger, not only passion or temperament determine our actions, but also circumstances. He continues: " . . . but it's also true that, in the same circumstances, with the same exterior stimuli, two people will react in different ways, according to their temperament, character, education . . . " (p. 155). The novelist puts this idea into practice with the family itself—each member undergoes the same situation, but reacts differently according to his own special characteristics.

In an interview concerning this novel, the author reaffirmed her interest in the Naturalistic technique: "Throughout the entire novel, we are presented with the struggle of heredity and environment trying to influence the formation of the personality of the protagonists."[15] One application of this theory is the adventuresome and travel-loving tendencies of the Rivero side of the family—traits which the children "inherit"—as opposed to the more bourgeois leanings of the Quintanas, embodied in the mother and Aunt Mag. Yet the author states clearly that both sides of the family contributed to the children's temperament: " . . . Lena, like Ger and like María, had inherited the innovating and adventurous spirit of the Riveros, but...there is no doubt that the conservative blood of the Quintanas also acted on them" (p. 133).

Miss Medio offers evidence outside of the family circle to prove her theory. Cheni, a rather dishonest boy who used to work for the Riveros, returns as a part of the group of revolutionaries and tries to steal some things from the house until Lena confronts him. This scene shows man's unchanging nature, and reinforces the idea that there has been no radical change of character throughout the novel. Each reacts to situations in a different way, but one can almost predict their actions.

The same references to the Rivero legend seem to fit into the pattern of Naturalistic theory, interpreted in a novel and rather sensational way. Several incidents connected directly or indirectly with the curse weighing on the Rivero family are left unexplained or undeveloped at the end of the novel. The first of these is the adventure Lena has with a gypsy who tells her fortune and offers the following prophecy: "Blood! I see blood on your hands, child. No one would say, looking at that ingenuous little face, that you would be capable of staining your hands with the blood of a man. And nevertheless, there is blood on your hands! And hands cannot lie. You will kill!" (p. 151). This startling news is later explained away insufficiently when Lena kills a chicken and stains her hands with blood. A variation on this very theme—the curse of the Riveros—reappears with the mysterious visit of a person about whom Lena had never heard: an old woman who identifies herself as Aunt Carina, Mr. Rivero's sister. Still more perplexing is the mother's reaction to the visit: she refuses to see "The Samaritan," as she calls Carina, and does not wish to accept the gifts of much-needed food the old woman has brought. Lena's attempts to clear up the enigma are in vain. Ger, who saw her at the family farm when he was seven, remembers some vague details; there are the usual references to the Rivero blood, but no further clarification. The disappearance of Ger and Heidi add still further mysteries which are never really resolved. These puzzling episodes are too strategic and the references to the curse too numerous to have been lapses on the part of the novelist. She obviously meant to place the reader and Lena Rivero in the same position at the end of the work in that, as in life, not all strings of the plot are neatly tied. In fact, the last words of the novel indicate clearly that Miss Medio intended to leave these aspects—all dealing with the ill luck of the Riveros—in the form of an open question as the story ends with a last reference to the mystery: "What could there be of truth in the curious legend that the Riveros dragged like a chain?" (p. 340).

The curse, which has seemed forced and overly melodramatic in a work of such realistic characteristics, is another way of manipulating this scientific-literary tenet of the late nineteenth century, Naturalism. That the author intends to orient the reader in this direction is made clear as Ger and Lena speak of the curse hanging over the family and the prophecy of the gypsy woman. Ger protests:

> The curse? . . . curse—how absurd! [. . .] Be careful, be very careful, my girl, about letting your fantasy run away! . . . We Riveros are like that . . . because . . . just because. Without fail. Let's accept the fact that we are a family that is a bit . . . extraordinary. A little picturesque, if you like. And let's admit that our restlessness has been transmitted from generation to generation, *as a hereditary sickness is transmitted* . . . (pp. 155–56, emphasis added)

Thus the "mystery" is robed in rather scientific terminology, but it could easily be interpreted as a simple way of adding sensationalism to the story—a suspicion shared by many critics.[16] Yet by accepting the idea of heredity which conditions the protagonists' reactions, we can better understand the fatality which hangs over their heads, and interpret the gypsy, Aunt Carina, and other minor episodes, as well as the disappearance of Heidi and Ger, as symbolic representations of the inalterable temperament inherited by the Riveros.

Character development, too, deliberately recalls techniques of the past century; Miss Medio does not choose to employ modern procedures of analysis through interior monologue, stream of consciousness, etc. Instead, there is an effort to make the habits and exterior of the character conform with the salient traits of his personality. The use of physical appearance or behavior to comment on one's inner life recalls techniques of characterization in the nineteenth century. Ger's exuberance and multiple interests are seen in his messy, disorderly room, whose contents reveal his own role as spokesman for progress (pp. 104–5; 258–59). María's soul, already dedicated to a religious life, finds expression in her neat room, which reflects an internal peace of spirit; her rejection of earthly things takes concrete form as she turns her dressing table into a miniature altar. Even her actions underline her single-minded dedication : she causes a scandal in the family by giving away a valuable watch. Heidi, on the other hand, has the normal interests in her numerous suitors, and uses her dressing table to full advantage.

The author identifies Mrs. Rivero with a piece of clothing that eventually indicates her status in the novel. It is the blue smock, symbol of her position as middle-class housewife and of her power in the family. The first introduction to the Riveros includes the following description of the mother: "Mrs. Rivero, owner of an elegant smock of blue velvet, adorned with black lace" (p. 19). Through repeated references, this piece becomes so much a part of her that it soon stands for the woman and the principles she upholds. When the children ask about Aunt Carina, " . . . they felt themselves intimidated, restrained by the melodramatic gesture of the thread-bare and proud blue smock . . . " (p. 225).

The author makes the difference between the family members as patent as possible, thus setting the stage for the contrast of individual temperament within a similar environment. A description of the Rivero children emphasizes this point: "The three—with a different goal to attain—strengthened their wings to hurl themselves to the conquest of space. María, toward such a high ideal, that her eyes were always fixed on Heaven. Ger gave himself over to a human ideal. As for Lena . . . her Franciscan humility was not a disguise, but a pause, a period of overcoming, on the road which led her to turn her dreams into reality" (p. 265).

Further contrast in personality becomes clear in two opposing movements which Miss Medio evolves through the characters in *We Riveros*. The presentation of Lena and Ger is based on dynamic growth and movement forward; they undergo experiences which mold their personalities in a visible manner. Even in María, the most placid of the children, one can see development in her strengthening of purpose. The characters' ability to adapt to change may be part of the scientific theories which Miss Medio uses in this novel; the application of this theory to young people makes it more plausible to chronicle such rapid changes and violent reactions, as well as the inevitable adjustments and compromises which the maturation process involves.

Other members of the family, however, undergo the same experience, but do not have the capacity or ability to change. I am referring to the two Quintanas—Mrs. Rivero and her sister Mag. Their age, traditional upbringing, and other factors have magnified the problems of adjustment to their new environment (the acceptance of poverty and the new era). If movement characterizes the children, complete inflexibility marks the attitudes of the older women. They are unable to initiate actions; they limit themselves to facing new situations with unyielding and indignant obstinacy.

IV   *Social Implications*

Mrs. Rivero is out of place and out of step with the new society; her unhappiness is a direct result of the refusal to accept the new situation by turning her home into a haven of traditional values. Suddenly, Mrs. Rivero's secure world becomes very unpredictable: her class status is gone, her economic security vanishes. She must relinquish her role as society hostess with the abandonment of the store. Her coterie, limited though it may have been, symbolized a coveted social position to her. The children, with the exception of the pious María, openly rebel at her old-fashioned ideas: Heidi runs away and is never heard of again; Ger's companions tend to the more radical kind; Lena refuses to become a lady. Yet instead of facing the situation, as the children do, Mrs. Rivero simply refuses to acknowledge that there has been more than a superficial change. Like the cat Kedi-Bey, she is not able to adjust to her new circumstances, and she, too, dies before the novel ends, an indication of her symbolic value, since the author's mother died later, during the Civil War.

Although the economic problems that beset most of the characters in Miss Medio's works are due, no doubt, to the privations suffered in her own life, the literary connection with similar themes in Galdós is tempting to explore. Each has investigated the reactions to sudden poverty in the bourgeoisie, a class which both writers see as holding an unstable position in society. Both contrast class attitudes, pointing to the importance of keeping up appearances in the middle class. Miss Medio analyzes this situation in *We Riveros*: the social position and aristocratic heritage of the upper class would not disappear even in poverty; the lower class was not ashamed to ask for help openly. Only the middle class, insecure in its social status, wary of what others might think or say, made great sacrifice to keep up the illusion of well-being. If her friends had continued their visits, Mrs. Rivero would have regaled them with the same prodigality as before (pp. 142–43).

Mrs. Rivero's major function in this work does not reside in her role as mother, but in her representation of a certain class and education during that period. She and her sister Mag were brought up in a comfortable bourgeois household, with every expectation of marrying into the same kind of family. Without doubt, much of her bitterness is due to the fact that her prospects did not materialize, that her husband was adventurous rather than stolid, and did not share her traditional outlook on the value of money. The split in ideology between the Quintana family and the Riveros is made quite plain by the author, as she contrasts the Quintana conservatism with the Riveros' adventurous spirit (p. 133).

Mrs. Rivero's upbringing has made her rigid, rather pretentious, and extremely conservative. She is a woman with strong convictions about duty and tradition, and therefore refuses to recognize the validity of change. This stubbornness is excusable while the family still has money, but her reaction to later situations which are distasteful or beyond her control is indicative of a class problem. Mrs. Rivero represents a prevalent type in the early twentieth century: the bourgeois woman who was not prepared to accept the sudden social and political upheavals of that period; the new freedom, the economic changes, the radical reevaluation of woman's position; the resultant insecurities are too much for this character to admit. Her upbringing, her conservative frame of mind, leave her totally unprepared to accept a new order, yet paradoxically, she is unable to conceive that her very lack is what the new reforms are trying to remedy.

Mrs. Rivero's inability to adjust to the new social change opens the novel to a wider scope of interpretation, in which the character may easily transcend his interest as an individual. This procedure fits perfectly into the ideal of the nineteenth-century novel; it also paves the way for the growing social awareness which Miss Medio develops in later works. Definite social injustices are aired in *We Riveros*: Mrs. Rivero's incapability of coping with the new problems becomes the fault of the social structure, for women were traditionally not prepared to accept responsibility for anything beyond household duties. Men, on the other hand, were unduly spoiled. Lena notes this unfair treatment and comments on the favoritism shown her brother: "Why doesn't Ger help us with the housework? Her sister answered her: 'Ah, no, Ger is a man, Ger has to study. He's the only man in the family and mama has to put all her hopes in him.' If she asked Aunt Mag, 'Why are you taking out the garbage? Give it to Ger . . . ' 'To him . . . ' answers Miss Quintana, scandalized—'Are you crazy?'" (p. 177).

Much of the social criticism stems from Lena's experiences and has to do with women's place in the world. Thus subjects variously aired include the exploitation of labor (at home, with women) and women's underprivileged status compared to men's. The character most aware of this problem is Ger, who brings it on himself to discuss with his reactionary mother the advantages of feminism and, much to her dismay, condones emancipation. From her statements, it is obvious that Mrs. Rivero has been conditioned to accept her position for so long that it is now impossible for her to understand the injustice of it; she reacts with horror to Ger's impassioned but logical plea that women be taught a profession. He points to the fate of spinsters, who need something to fill an emotional and perhaps economic void (p. 179), yet even in the light of empirical evidence, his mother remains adamant:

> Mrs. Rivero adored Ger. . . . Only on one difficult point did Mrs. Rivero show herself to be irreducible: on whatever had to do with girls and the impositions of modern life. She educated her daughters as she had been educated: to rule a home. She felt aversion toward mannish women, whom she qualified as suffragettes and defended with all her strength what she called delicateness, femininity in woman. If woman left her house to earn a living, the concept of the traditional home would disappear . . . (p. 180)

Although the family is in desperate need of money, Mrs. Rivero is appalled at Ger's suggestion that her daughters work as usherettes in one of the theaters. "You're crazy, my son, you are mad! For this I brought you up like royalty?" (p. 183).

Ger has the privilege of a clearer vision than the others, and he makes the final indictment of their situation, again removing it from a personal level to give it a wider frame of reference: the problem of the middle class and its resultant implications: "No, mother, I'm not reproaching you, but rather this stupid society in which we move. The aristocracy can permit itself the luxury of living as it wishes. The lower class solves its problems in its own way. But the middle class, the long-suffering and vain middle class, more loaded with prejudices than with money, lives a false and often terrible life . . ." (p. 182).

Practical illustrations of Ger's statement abound throughout the novel. Mrs. Rivero's unhappy situation is the prime example, but Aunt Mag runs a close second: her lack of practical education left her unprepared to help the family during the period of crisis. She had learned how to tat and embroider, but practical skills, such as keeping accounts, were a mystery to her (p. 280). Not content with these two outstanding examples, Ger offers further proof as he points to a family of five unmarried women, who, if they do not get husbands, will be incapable of support after their father's death, since they know no trade. He likewise feels that women of the middle class should not be sheltered, because it produced unpleasant results later on. Lena faints after seeing blood when she kills a chicken; Ger comments, "For children in the country, sacrificing an animal is a natural thing. They see them born and die and bear offspring and mate . . . They are better prepared than we to face life, because they live in contact with Nature. . . . Because of this they are healthier, they suffer fewer complexes than we . . . " (p. 254). He goes on to compare this to the arranged marriage, where the bride, who often has not even spoken to her prospective husband alone, does not know what to expect on her wedding night (p. 255).

Such interest in social prejudices and injustices falls mainly in the category of women's rights, since they obviously stem from the realms of personal experience.

V   We Riveros: *Spain and its History*

These experiences become fictionalized material only as a first step; a second transforms them into generalizations which include the wider frame of reference mentioned above. As such, the novelist uses the environment (specifically Oviedo), a picture of the middle class, and finally, an historical overlay as integral ingredients of the novel. History becomes a concrete and powerful force which acts directly on the protagonists. It provides a chronicle of the times, but the choice of period is doubly appropriate since the freedom symbolized by the advent of the Second Republic and the resultant rejection of the Monarchy (symbol of the parental image) simultaneously parallel Lena's individual freedom. Events of the decade from 1924 to 1934 were especially violent in Oviedo: the black market, strikes, house searches, hunger and terror, street fighting and bombs marked the 1930's in the north of Spain. History interests the author because of the continual change and movement which necessarily affect the individual, and just as we find contrast of character in the static older generation and the dynamic children, there are also opposing forces on a deeper level: history as opposed to *intrahistory* (another point of contact with Galdós).[17]

The third strong contrast appears in descriptions of Oviedo, which, like history, makes its presence felt with a force that also molds, enhances, or emphasizes character development. The city's special personality is made manifest as sections alternate between family problems and Oviedo, confronting character in the Riveros with the old and new in the city. The amount of material devoted to Oviedo gives it a strategic place in the novel. The numerous investigations into its special character do not directly concern the story, but reinforce the background—for example, the disquisition on class structure and especially on emigration and the bourgeois merchant prepares the reader for the entrance of the Rivero family (p. 47).

Given the symbolic value of the characters in *We Riveros*, and their position within the historical framework of their country, it is a logical step to move to an interpretation of the family as a symbol of Spain itself. Like the Riveros, Spain is formed of generations linked by blood, but also like the family, the country has suffered under an unavoidable curse of violence which seems to be an unhappy combination of temperament and circumstance. The mother represents extreme traditional values; Ger, the liberal ones. Even well-known Spanish types are in this work: the *indiano* (the father, who emigrates to America and returns), the old spinster who lives with the family (Aunt Mag), the woman who dedicates herself to the Church early in life (María). Lena views all of this from the dual perspective of the past (her childhood) and the present (her return to her birthplace). She tries to find an explanation for the Riveros' (and Spain's) history, but there is no answer. Her pilgrimage to Oviedo has stirred up memories, but offered no solutions.

CHAPTER 5

New Directions

W HEN *Funcionario público* (*Public Servant*) appeared, it was apparent that Miss Medio had written an unqualified success.[1] Although only three years separated it from *We Riveros*, the radical change in subject matter, the purpose, the point of view, and even the form revealed a new facet to the author's approach to literature, yet the human understanding that gave her first work its appeal remained. From a narrow provincial focus, Miss Medio moves the setting to Madrid; the maturing, inquiring mind of Lena Rivero, who ideally had her horizons open to her and her life ahead of her, is replaced with a middle-aged failure; the author substitutes for the curious and penetrating glance of late adolescence the problems of everyday life—economic, social, marital—and raises them to an unmistakably social level.

I Public Servant, *Part I*

Pablo Marín, the protagonist, works as a telegraph operator in Madrid, barely making enough money to live decently. Decently, that is, if you consider pinching pennies, living as a sublessee and dreaming of success a satisfactory way of life. He is nondescript; he could be any one of hundreds of people. "He is a man of average height, of regular features. Agreeable, altogether. He dresses modestly. Almost carelessly. In order to appreciate that, one has only to see the dirty collar of his gabardine coat. It's a very worn gabardine" (pp. 12–13). This description provides the reader with some basic facts about Marín: a colorlessness which shades into anonymity (with such words as *average*, *regular*, and the lack of adjectives granting him a distinctive status), his economic condition, and his apathy (his negligence as to his clothes, his soiled collar). Pablo dreams of bettering his situation, but his hopes tend to be unrealistic: winning a lottery or a bet. His fantasies suddenly become objectified when he finds some papers on the street belonging to a young woman, Natalia Blay. He tries to track her down, with rather ambivalent feelings about discovering what Natalia is really like, but her inaccessibility converts her into a symbol of all he longs for, but cannot obtain.

This mysterious woman is a contrast to his wife Teresa, whose private dreams center around an apartment of their own. Their life seems to be harder on her, since she can measure her time in the monotony of their existence and the recognition of her husband's failure. She is completely resigned: Pablo is predictably unvarying in his jokes, manners and opinions, she begins to lose hope of the excitement and economic ease that she feels should be part of life.

Pablo's personal life, aggravated by worries about money, is far from happy. His sexual inadequacy (which Dolores Medio hints at but does not develop) seems to be the direct result of his other inadequacies, and the physical correlative of his failure in marriage. Yet he refuses to see the imminent tragedy in their relationship, which is marked by a lack of understanding on both sides and the inability to communicate with each other. One example will suffice: Teresa, upset about life in the apartment, cries bitterly, telling Pablo that they must leave immediately. Instead of trying to understand the reasons behind this outburst (which go far beyond the present situation), "His sight strays from that form who shakes sobbing on the bedspread, to the plate in which the last spoonfuls of broth are getting cold. And the soup is very good. Teresa knows how to give it a certain bit of seasoning which almost turns it into a delicacy. He sits down again and finishes eating it, tipping the dish covertly, to get even the last drop" (p. 176). His insensitivity, combined with Teresa's growing scorn, will lead to the inevitable breakup of the marriage.

Pablo's first attempts to locate Natalia Blay soon become a serious matter, although even he is not aware of its significance: the woman constitutes an exciting goal, a possible conquest which injects new excitement into his life. Suddenly he shaves and puts on a clean shirt—a marked contrast to the numerous references to his, or Teresa's negligence—and "accidentally" forgets to mention the documents to his wife. His adventures in trying to find the mysterious woman alternate with descriptions of his feeling about work, or his discussions with his fellow workers about their view of life. His own moments of illumination—the realization that he has been dehumanized into a cog of the machine that is society (p. 91)— bring momentary rebellion, symbolized by crumpling and hurling down a telegram, but true to his character, he is unable to sustain any positive action and settles back to his work, dreaming about possible raises.

Thus the reader is presented with two distinct but equally important sides of the same person: Pablo in his role in society, as a public servant, and Pablo the man, whose private self is revealed by his dreams and his relationship with his wife. His basic problem is the inability of these two aspects to coexist in harmony, for there is a great distance between objective and subjective reality. He evades reality whenever possible—the only form of rebellion possible for a man with his characteristics. His fascination with Natalia is a form of escape, for Natalia-person is not as crucial as Natalia-symbol, the object of his dreams. Another more short-lived hope is the lottery, which he loses, but he is afraid to tell Teresa, who does not understand that the two hundred *pesetas* is an investment in escape: "Teresa doesn't understand [. . .] that the price is small if one takes into account that I've bought the right to dream for almost three months" (p. 105). Instead of facing the present and adjusting his sights to reality, he prefers to look forward to unknown pleasures, and he dreams of his new wealth winning back Teresa's affections: He mentally savors Teresa's joy and love as he plunks down his winning ticket, her tears, and their second honeymoon (pp.107–8).

Yet if the recognition of his personal failure encourages him to take an escape route in his private life—objectified and polarized by the reality of Teresa and the dream of Natalia Blay—his life outside his home, that of man as a social being, offers no more satisfying possibilities. He realizes that he has a place in society, as a small cog in a huge machine:

What happens when children take apart a plaything to find what it has inside? They forget to put the pieces back in their place and there are pieces left over. Also men, when they play at seeing what this infernal machine of society has inside, become perplexed when they reconstruct it. [. . .] As for the gears, who notices them? Marín the cog. López the cog. Miralles the cog. . . . All off the assembly line, the same thing. Easy to replace when they break down. (p. 95)

Thus there is another aspect to Pablo the individual: the anonymous man, whose function it is to serve society and who is determined by it. Pablo rebels against this dehumanizing conception which ignores the uniqueness of each person, yet, true to his character, he cannot translate momentary defiance into positive action: "But, at times, one can't avoid this movement of rebellion. Alright, but rebellion against whom, against what? Against society? Against life? Could I really be a misfit [*inadaptado*], a troublemaker, almost dangerous for the community? I believe I'm exaggerating. My rebellion is peaceful. Inoffensive. Rather, I would say discontent, inconvenience. Weariness. Disgust . . ." (p. 93).

His "social" life is perfectly represented by his job, in which automatic movements have replaced any human interest in his work, for years of the same motions and despair of any novelty have worn away his attention. The peripheral activities also connected with his job are completely mechanical—the same time of arising, the same routine of dressing, route of the subway, and finally his job. Interesting too, is the fact that he did not choose his profession. Apparently he wanted to farm, but his mother insisted that a white-collar job would bring more money and be more prestigious. Thus both aspects of his life are unsatisfactory; in the words of the author, Pablo is an *inadaptado*—unable to adapt to his circumstances.

If Pablo could be described as maladjusted, Teresa's adjective would be *embittered*. She no longer has faith in her husband, whom she now considers as more of an object than a person: "I love Pablo because . . . because I love him. Because one also becomes attached to a dog" (p. 78). She has gone one step further than her husband, because her more limited outlook on life and her natural attachment to reality have made her realize that Pablo's hopes for a raise in salary are no more than daydreams, promises without hope of being fulfilled: "But Teresa doesn't say anything because the weariness of facing the same monotonous reality each day has even taken from her the strength to rebel" (p. 23). Just as Natalia Blay is the objective correlative for Pablo's daydreams, Teresa thinks of a former boyfriend, now a successful doctor, and imagines herself as his wife, rich in affection and money.

An ironic note ends the first part of the novel: Pablo imagines in detail a scene in which he comes home and announces his success in the lottery. Since he does not have the winning ticket, this hope is also dashed, but when he arrives home, the scene is enacted almost as he thought, but with the roles reversed: Teresa has won a sewing machine. Not content to leave things on this optimistic note, however, Dolores Medio ends the section with Pablo's fury: their landlady refuses to allow them to bring the machine into their room.

II   Public Servant, *Part II*

A police inspector, intrigued by Pablo's search, offers to help him find Natalia, but Pablo hurriedly refuses, and the following important key to his personality explains the reason: "In his little life in which colorless days, pounded in the mortar of a prosaic reality, are wired together, the invisible presence of Natalia is a myth, which feeds his fantasy. [. . .] He takes refuge in her, against his will, as Teresa does in the memory of a man whom she despises, but who is, in spite of himself, the contrast, the escape from her small world, which doesn't offer her any surprise" (p. 134). Pablo prefers the delicious limbo between finding and not finding her.

His constant visits to the paralytic Guzmán, who once knew Natalia Blay (she refused to marry him), provide an outlet for Pablo's own feelings. At his first meeting, Guzmán's domineering manner and powerful physique remind him of Michelangelo's Moses, and he thinks of him as "the Boss." Guzmán represents an older way of life, in which man was measured by his individual worth. This kind of person is now useless in today's modern world, just as Guzmán's legs can no longer function, and when the older man complains of present-day conditions, Pablo "also feels nostalgia for the old days and fears that the world has become materialized, mechanized to excess" (p. 142).

The economic pressures tighten on Pablo and Teresa, and the everpresent theme of money—or lack of it—appears full force on contrasting planes: the generalized and the individual. The economic problems of Madrid as a whole in the postwar years come to the fore in a cross-section of people and their attitudes toward money. The public servant receives such a meagre salary that it is almost impossible to raise a family on what he earns (attested by the discussions between Pablo and his co-workers). Others are willing to sell themselves or their principles for the right price: Mrs. Rufa, the landlady, raises their rent, knowing that they cannot pay it, because she has a good offer for their room. It will ostensibly become an office, but it is understood that the secretary and her employer will extend their working hours into the night. Mrs. Rufa thus allows the tone of her apartment to decline: "Pablo Marín understands, and his soul begins to be filled with bitterness by that miserable prostitution. The wave of infamy and misery was now reaching even here, even to honorable houses. A few more cents and the old lady sold her soul to the devil" (p. 175).[2]

On the individual level—the second element of the contrast— Pablo's reduced circumstances cause reality to intrude into his dream life, and the forced move reveals to him the true extent of their poverty. This is the price of honesty, and it is a defect in Teresa's eyes: "You're born honorable like you're born stupid. It's inevitable" (p. 174). His dream world thus centers on a nebulous future raise, which he embroiders to suit his fancy.

The hunt for a new apartment is a dramatic series of ups and downs for the Marín family. The clean modern rooms that attract Teresa are out of the question because of the price; lodgings within their price range are really undesirable. What starts out as an adventure turns into a sharp disappointment, frustrating to them both and proving that there is no possibility of moving from their level on Pablo's present salary. Thus the tempting opportunity to share a modern apartment with another young couple vanishes, because the price—fifteen hundred *pesetas*—is triple what they can afford. Their odyssey becomes a failure; finally they get a room much like their old one, thus marking no significant change, except perhaps downward. Teresa, unhappy with the neighbors, and utterly bored, expresses the first thought of leaving her husband: "She thinks at times that it would be a solution to go away to her home town. To change the scene. To stop seeing Pablo for a while. To abandon that poor and dirty life together" (p. 212).

Dolores Medio prepares the reader for Pablo's next failure. In an excellent chapter which alternates thoughts about his forthcoming raise—now a certainty—with snatches of the article he is reading, the author builds up his excitement about breaking the good news to Teresa. His "scene" is all planned, but like the last "dream scene" (the lottery), this one does not materialize either. He opens the door to an empty room, with an envelope awaiting him on the table. Teresa's abandonment finally shakes him to the point that he suddenly sees the truth about life and the reality of his personal existence. He realizes that the fault did not lie in deprivation, but in his very attitude toward life; "The night when Mrs. Rufa got rid of us, I discovered the real reason for her desperation [. . .] Our poverty. A moral poverty more terrible than the physical poverty" (p. 236). Wandering through the city, thinking of his situation and that of others, he walks onto a bridge and hits the railing with rage. A stranger sees him and takes him to a bar, buys him drinks, and tells him about his own unhappy situation—he is out of a job and his wife supports him. This makes Pablo realize that he still has something left: his job. He shakes the man's hand, thanks him, and rushes to catch a bus, because he has only twenty minutes before his shift starts. His return toward the city, which he had left in his wandering, symbolizes his submission to society, and the end of another short-lived rebellion.

III *Pablo Marín, Social Entity*

Public Servant falls easily into the category of the social novel, that popular breed of literature diffused in Spain during the 1950's and characterized by a relatively realistic treatment of the subject, a desire to suggest reform or point out abuses of the social system, and the use of a character as representative of a class, which, however, does not preclude the individualizing of character. Typical examples of the social novel can be seen in such works as López Pacheco's *Central eléctrico* (*Electric Powerhouse*), 1958, or López Salinas' *La Mina* (*The Mine*), 1960, both of which use rural or provincial settings. Enrique Azcoaga's *El empleado* (*The Employee*), 1949, and Zunzunegui's *Esta oscura desbandada* (*This Dark Disbandment*), 1952, come close to *Public Servant* because of the urban theme.

Although Dolores Medio does not neglect Pablo Marín as an individual (this aspect is developed through his private life, his relationship with his wife, his personal problems and dreams), she obviously feels it of importance to stress the other side of the character: Pablo as a representative of a specific segment of society. To this end, she has literally transferred her philosophy concerning man's place in the modern world to *Public Servant*:

Man—the character in a novel—does not exist outside of the social framework. Modern life has turned him into a cog and he must fit into the place in the machine which has been allotted to him. Any attempt at rebellion, any process which turns him into a maladjusted person, destroys him, reduces him to a piece of useless scrap-iron which society throws on the dump. His private life, even his intimate life [. . .] is influenced, or rather, determined, by social factors, and he must allow himself to be dragged along by the current or be destroyed in a heroic but sterile iso-lation.[3]

That Pablo must be considered as a member of a social class is evident from the title—his significance resides equally in the role as public servant. The colorless description, his very averageness, makes his outlines indistinct in a way that sacrifices his individuality the more easily to identify him as a representative of a group. His job determines his existence, and this gives the author a chance to point to low salaries which do not take into account the cost of living or the number of members of a family, or the impassivity of the government toward his plight.

To this end, she deliberately situates one chapter (Chapter 28) in Pablo's office in order to concentrate on the views of several of Pablo's co-workers, who at that time are discussing the tempting possibility of a raise. Here is where Pablo begins to discover that even though the office workers are viewed primarily as part of a unit, each one is also an individual in his own right. A little probing into others' personalities gives interesting results:

> Pablo Marín observes Mariana Gil curiously. He begins to discover her this morning. Until today, Mariana Gil was for him "Orense" [the place to which she sent telegrams] just as he would be "Valencia" for those who did not treat him individually. [. . .] He looks around. In this beehive where men move in time to mechanical work, with hardly any contact among themselves, he could discover—he is sure of it—a good variety and richness of feelings, of interesting lives. (—Each man, a world—he says to himself—. True. A great truth. A wheel, a gear, a name on a file card, but also a life. Perhaps a little life marvelous in its simplicity [. . .] (p. 223)

But, as usual, another worker really articulates this idea, disagreeing violently with the idea of all for the good of society: "—Collectivity, collectivity. Keep your damned collectivity! The world seems to have forgotten, nowadays, that man is something more than a number, than a figure. He is an individual. He is a being who thinks, who has his own reactions and feelings" (p. 225). Clearly there is a protest—mild though it may be—against man's dehumanization in an impersonal and mechanized world, symbolized by the office. Suddenly shadowy figures come to life, each bearing the stamp of his uniqueness, each with problems similar to those of Pablo.

The other side of the argument also has its spokesman: a co-worker, Leo Miralles, and others insist that man is actually a number and nothing more, and his main function therefore is to serve society. One example of man at the mercy of the state is forced retirement, a practice which automatically proclaims his uselessness at a given time. Pablo compares this to the Eskimo custom of condemning old people to death (pp. 88–89); and further establishes analogies with the "programmed" citizens of Aldous Huxley's *Brave New World*. During his brief moment of rebellion, Pablo recognizes that he may be maladjusted, but it is best to put these thoughts out of his mind: "OK. No more thinking. Turn off your brain, Pablo. Turn off your brain and life. I mean, vegetate. More comfortable, of course. Worry? Why, if after all . . ." (pp. 93–94). Yet there is always a residual dissatisfaction as he thinks that he would like to be a Robinson Crusoe and live away from society (p. 91), and looking at the Communications Building, he can imagine "hundreds of public servants, synchronized in their common effort, [who] move the machinery of this giant monster, which extends its invisible tentacles over lands and seas. Each one of the men who work within it is like a gear, like a wheel" (p. 91). His rebellion, of course, is simply a mental reaction against the situation; as stated above, it is not within his character to take any positive steps toward remedying the wrongs he sees. Friends at the telegraph office have the same economic problems as Pablo, but two of them, who represent dramatically antithetic solutions which Pablo *could* take, solve these problems in ways that Pablo cannot. Sixto Magnet is a bachelor, which relieves him of family responsibilities. No ties hold him down. He supplements his salary by dishonest means, but his freedom, his economic ease, his sexual conquests, make him an object of reluctant admiration among his friends. Pablo's dreams of Natalia are no doubt built partially on Sexto's tales of his amorous exploits.

Developed as character-contrast to Magnet, and presented as another of the possibilities of choice open to Pablo, is Leo Miralles, a man burdened with a large family and a small income. This person is one of the few sympathetic characters in the novel, in his positive attitude toward life. Like Pablo, he refuses to rebel, but this position is not due to indecision. Miralles is truly optimistic, with an acceptance of life that approaches a boyish spontaneity. He believes that one's attitude will determine his fate: if he smiles at life, it will smile back. "Perhaps life was only that: a miracle. A miracle of will, that not everyone understood or accepted. That poor devil did.

His optimism, his smile, were the acceptance of the marvelous gift, and in turn, the demand that the gift be realized in all of its bounty" (p. 74). Antithetical terms describe this attitude: heroism on a small scale. Miralles is the anomaly here, in his uncomplaining acceptance of what life holds for him. To make him the more outstanding, Miss Medio employs somewhat exaggerated descriptive terms when explaining his attitudes (he is the only one in the novel who enjoys such a privilege). He has "a giant's stature," and seems like "a hero of peace, who, anonymously, wins the daily battle for existence without crosses or medals" (p. 74). His unfailing optimism, his seemingly harmless exterior, covers a will of iron, and the stuff that heroes—or saints—are made of, for he believes that one can make of life what one wishes by a kind of positive thinking: "It's necessary to smile at life so it will smile back at us" (p. 74).

Miralles' willingness to conform also affects his role in society. He believes that man must consider himself as part of the social machine, for society itself will make us adjust our sights to fit into a more general scheme. "Society is like a river, which polishes and polishes the edges of our rebelliousness until it turns us into smooth, round pebbles. Then and only then do we fit into its bed perfectly. Without causing trouble. People who are maladjusted or rebellious are generally dangerous for the life of the community (p. 75). As previously observed, Pablo's inability to adapt to the social situation, unlike Miralles', is, of course, a main theme of the novel. Further character contrasts, representing the insuperable distance between the realm of possibility and that of the unattainable (given Pablo's personality), are the pair of older men, Guzmán and Irueta. Guzmán, as has been established, is independent, wealthy, and master of his own world, limited though it may be. Pablo admires his force and decisiveness in the same way he feels about Sixto Magnet; Guzmán embodies an economic and personal ideal which Pablo can never realize.

Irueta suggests the probable evolution of the order-minded Leo Miralles. Irueta represents the future of the public servant, whose fate is in the hands of an impersonal machine which does not recognize human merit, and only measures service in terms of time periods. At this time, he is trying to arrange for his pension, which will provide hardly any money: "Even for this, one has to go in circles. You know, for a matter of twenty days I lost my promotion. I hardly have anything left. Bah! A pittance" (p. 84). Furthermore, he is burdened with five unmarried daughters. Pablo quickly draws the parallel, seeing himself in the same position:

> He ends up by confessing to himself that Máximo Irueta's anguish is his own. He begins to see himself in twenty, in thirty years, walking along Alcalá street, weighed down with the burden of his work, now useless: So many years of service. So many thousands of extra hours. So many projects. Everything puts its own weight on his shoulders. Nevertheless, all that can be reduced to a few facts, dates. [...] A handshake by the bosses. Perhaps a banquet organized by one's companions. And one less on the roster. The same thing he once thought about those who were leaving, leaving a vacant place for promotion." (p. 90)

Teresa and Natalia offer another contrasting pair: Teresa, embittered, a symbol of Pablo's impotence, silently accusing him of failure. Natalia, because she is not real, can represent anything Pablo wishes and thus develops into an exciting adventure, a future conquest and a hope for something which Pablo did not have before. These two women add to the interpretation of man as an individual in relation with others.

IV *Pablo Marín, Individual vs. Society*

The epigraph to the work shows Dolores Medio's insistence on the whole person, for although the generic title of the novel and the problems of the government employee orient the reader toward the social implications of the work, further study probes the conflict within the individual character and his problems within the wider scope of the employment system. Borrowing from the works of her fellow Asturian, Pérez de Ayala, Dolores Medio begins the book with a phrase that points to the dual nature of man: " . . . since he is an animal endowed with spirit, man always tends to be in civil war with himself." Much of the novel develops this very point: Marín, in conflict with dissatisfaction with his job and with his unhappy home life (a partial product of his job), must balance the two sides of his life. The sad conclusion is that he finds satisfaction in neither place, and must turn to daydreams in order to compensate for the miserable existence at home and at work.

Although the author alternates episodes between the personal and the social world—typified by Pablo's home and office life—and further polarizes them through symbols represented by contrasting pairs (Teresa-Natalia, Miralles-Magnet, Guzmán-Irueta), the two have a symbiotic relationship which forms the root of Pablo's problems. He represents a class as well as an individual, and it is man in his dual role that Dolores Medio analyzes. Pablo is unable to adjust, the author suggests, but his problem is that he is maladjusted in both roles, and that the socioeconomic problems aggravate the personal ones : his sense of failure and Teresa's scorn for him are in direct ratio to the amount of money he brings home. Money, therefore, denotes power, success, and ultimately, happiness, as personified by Sixto Magnet. Ironically, this paragon of success is unmasked as dishonest and commits suicide, thus revealing the falseness of monetary standards of "success."

The struggle between the individual as such and the mass man he represents continues as a leitmotif throughout the novel, ending in the supplantation of the individual in favor of the worker. Leo Miralles stands for the local employee, continually suggesting that man is part of society and it is his duty to adapt to it. Although the idea is repugnant to Pablo, he too must admit that he is a representative of a certain class of person: "But he, what could he do to help it? That's life. His problem is the problem of many families who live in these same conditions. There's no reason to despair" (p. 16). Unfortunately, Pablo turns this incipient solidarity into an excuse to explain away his own failure.

Unlike Miralles, Pablo and Teresa let the economic problem color their personal lives. Their lack of will power and the refusal to face life on its own terms condition their personal philosophy. On the most intimate level, Pablo's problem of impotency is directly related to his sense of failure, his fear of having children in a place they are unwanted (the apartment), and his inability to provide for them adequately. This attitude of resentful resignation in turn affects Teresa and demoralizes the couple. The collar of Pablo's coat is dirty (p. 13); the two eat on a slightly soiled tablecloth with napkins in the same condition; the two plates are slightly chipped on the edges (p. 21). There are still further signs of the apathy into which they both have sunk: "One morning I couldn't find my razor. Like today, it was a day of rationing. There was no hot water. I left without shaving and . . . well, nothing happened. Teresa didn't even protest. It wasn't worth it. Also she had stopped brushing her hair. Just about around that time." (p. 27). The parallels between the physical and mental condition are all too evident: both states show signs of the degeneration which is the result of hopelessness.

Both characters are bitter or unable to change the situation. They live in a state of abulia which the author describes perfectly: the inability to act decisively in order to better their lot. They invariably blame their poverty on bad luck. Pablo, remembering how their early plans never materialized, thinks "Well, but am I to blame for it? No, sir. Only luck. Lousy luck. Even fate influences this" (p. 22). He later voices the same feeling: "Cards? What cards has destiny given me? [My duties at the office], a miserable salary and a stupid wife, who thinks I'm incapable of having an affair" (p. 54). The same blindness which prevents him from seeing the dissolution of his marriage also prevents him from realizing that the true cause of his failure lies within himself.

Pablo's main problem is his inability to control his life. His indecisiveness is the quality which is the other determinant of his existence; he is constantly dominated by circumstances. His solution is to daydream of the future, but even introspection, an inward form of action, is not to his liking. With the same kind of scientific intent as in *We Riveros*, the author studies a certain personality and its reactions to a given situation. The idea of determinism is even stronger in *Public Servant* than in the first novel, for the end of the work places the protagonist exactly where he started when the novel opened, except for the loss of his wife. Various episodes emphasize his weak character: his embarrassment when buying flowers for Natalia (he insists that they are for his daughter), (p. 42). His inquiries at the hotel show his nervousness and insecurity. Having learned that Natalia is there no longer, he presses the flowers onto a beggar woman rather than bring them home and have to explain them to his wife.

Natalia Blay symbolizes Pablo's mute rebellion against the mediocrity of his life, the last cry of a man who will never have any real adventures. She can provide a romantic note in the otherwise monotonous existence: She is a person, an individual, and not a simple list of facts (the reaction of the police inspector, p. 132). Her physical absence indicates that Pablo will never break the circle of his own mediocrity, but the fact that she represents the unattainable makes the enigma almost desirable. She provides the daydream on which Pablo can spend his fantasies, and her very indistinctness, which connotes everything he cannot have, tantalizes him.

V   *Style and Themes*

Public Servant is basically a realistic novel, but rather than concentrate on the usual details of exterior reality (as she did in *We
Riveros*), Dolores Medio chooses a more interior realism: the study
of a man placed in an environment to which he cannot adapt. Since
the main interest resides in Pablo and his problems with adjustment,
the stylistic emphasis must focus on the man within his milieu and
his reaction to it. There is hardly a description; his own thoughts
transmit his self-image. The reader is therefore limited to a narrow
viewpoint composed of Pablo's musings, random comments by
the author, and the opinion of the only other person whose thoughts
are revealed to us: Teresa.

Just as the traditional form in *We Riveros* was a structural device
to reinforce the impact of the work, so the more experimental format
of *Public Servant* is Dolores Medio's deliberate effort to complement
contemporary problems with more modern techniques. There is,
for example, an interesting interior monologue which alternates
with an objective account from a sports page Pablo is reading:

(Now the football world is beginning to stir because of the world cham-
pionships, and as for Spain and her game with Turkey . . .) The restless
voice jumps [from] behind the word, playing hide-and-seek with Pablo
Marín: (Turkey . . . "The Disenchanted" of Pierre Loti. . . . Mystery. . . .
An attractiveness, of course. . . . Natalia, an unknown woman. . . . A
woman who is not yours, Pablo Marín. Your friends. The comments. . . .
You criticize Sixto Magnet, but you envy him. Magnet is a man, you say.
And why? Because of his business? Because he has a woman. . . ? (p. 19)

Most of Dolores Medio's art consists of an emphasis on character
development, for she has always preferred the concrete to the abstract, the example to the problem. Thus each character of any significance in *Public Servant* represents the application of the inference.
By polarizing the attitudes within the complementary pairs (Miralles'
unselfishness contrasted to Magnet's egoism, for example), Miss
Medio can easily suggest alternatives to the reader without having
to reinforce her point with a great deal of prefatory information.
Although each has a life of his own, he functions mainly to give
another perspective to Pablo's existence. In addition to these major
characters, the author paints very human portraits of other people
who appear and disappear quickly. She is a master at the quick

incisive touch, bringing the character to life with deft strokes, preferring to emphasize pathetic qualities to arouse the reader's sympathy. One example of her technique is the description of the beggar woman upon whom Pablo thrusts the useless bouquet of flowers he bought for Natalia:

> Pablo looks at the woman with curiosity. She is still young. She could have been beautiful. Now her face is prematurely faded and her belly bulges, announcing an imminent motherhood. [. . .] Next to the luxury of the young, well-dressed women who pass by her side, the misery of that humble girl stands out more; she expects a child and sells tobacco and matches on the edge of the sidewalk. [. . .] "Take them, ma'am. I'm giving them to you. Don't look so frightened. They are for you. You can sell them, if you want. If you like flowers, you can keep them." [. . .] She is bewildered. She wants to say something to him. To thank him. But Pablo is already crossing the street and the woman laughs and cries, clutching against her chest, against her full belly, that strange gift of a man who called her ma'am and has given something to her without asking anything in return. The woman's face has lit up, and looks younger." (p. 51)

Other portraits built on similar emotional content are the crazy old lady whom the Maríns visit in their search for new quarters, and the final description of the man who, although he is in great unhappiness himself, still finds time to help and pity another human being.

Reactions to *Public Servant* were expectedly varied. Critics were most interested in this work because they felt it would signal the direction that the Nadal winner would take and would, in some measure, justify Miss Medio's career. One reviewer, A. Valencia, felt that Marín was not developed at all, and sensed the strong presence of the novelist behind her character.[4] Yet adverse reactions were in the minority; most critics felt that *Public Servant* was a decided advance over the first work, and that, although they recognized invariables from *We Riveros*—especially the author's sympathetic attitude, the humor which helped to lighten the novel somewhat, the "humanness" of the characters, and the preference for middle-class subjects—they were most pleased with her new approach to the novel.[5]

Although her technique is modernized and her theme conforms to the tendencies of contemporary literature and the social novel, it is interesting to note that the subject itself and Miss Medio's sources of information are not exactly innovational. Miss Medio's methods of gathering data for her book recall the procedures of the nineteenth-century novelist. She worked as a substitute for a short while at the telegraph office, thereby meeting the workers and hearing their problems. Thus documented in "atmosphere," she felt fully competent to draw on her own experience to use as a basis for the work.[6]

Her main character, too, recalls a popular subject in the previous century. The civil servant made his debut as a character in his own right in the nineteenth century. Writers even then posed the questions of an economic problem, signaling as well the favoritism and low salaries which were the pitfalls of this position. Pérez Galdós' novel *Meow* treats the predicament of the *cesante*—the public employee who has been dismissed—and follows his desperate attempts to be rehired so he can retire on a pension. In more recent times, the playwright Carlos Muñiz in *El tintero* (*The Inkwell*), 1961, caricatured the dehumanized attitude of big business toward the worker, and the grotesque irony of a company that refuses to accept its employee as an individual with human needs. Azcoaga's *The Employee* (1949) treats the employee in much the same way as Dolores Medio in developing the irreconcilable split between individual and worker.

The problems of the sublessee have been presented as a theme in contemporary Spanish literature on a par with the economic privations in postwar Madrid. An offshoot of the unstable economic situation, a shortage of inexpensive housing forced young couples to realize that in Madrid the longed-for apartment would have to remain in the planning stage for a while. These people, whose salaries could not provide enough to allow them a place to themselves, often rented a room in a larger apartment which would hold several families, all sharing kitchen and bathroom privileges. Thus the very number and variety of people provided an author with a tempting microcosm of contemporary society, and he often treated it as such. One thinks of Zunzunegui's *This Dark Disbandment*, a novel whose date (1952) attests to the immediacy of the problem. An effective theatrical exposition of the same situation appeared in 1960 with *La Madriguera* (*The Lair*) by Ricardo Rodríguez Buded, a play which gives equal importance to a number of characters living in this kind of situation. Miss Medio's personal experience must have provided the inspiration for the general outlines of the problem, which she develops in later works. Speaking of this, she states, "I lived as a sublessee for nine years in Madrid . . . The life of the sublessee is very sad, because he cannot have anything at his disposal. Everything is shared with other tenants: bath, kitchen, toilet. Man's natural passions become exasperated in this terrible life together, in this forced intimacy, as hard as it is sad, in which one has to share everything under conditions that approach wretchedness." [7]

Pablo and Teresa share the apartment with three families. They have a small room to themselves, and fixed hours for bathroom and kitchen privileges. The atmosphere of the place is far from pleasant; a certain hostility, partially born of the desperate knowledge that each is forced to live here, is evident in the relationships among the families, and the author describes this mood as the "hostile atmosphere of the sublessee" (p. 25). Close living also brings out petty rancors and jealousy. Miss Medio penetrates the special psychology of the women living there in the episode of the silver salt cellar : after one woman displays hers, each of the others feels the necessity to own one too. It personifies the struggle for status, for approval, and for individuality that communal living deprives these people of.

In *Public Servant*, Dolores Medio has made a major change in subject matter and novelistic technique. She has moved from the world of feminine adolescence to the broader scope of social questions and individual problems of failure. Her Naturalism has become less melodramatic and more sociologically oriented: the forces against which Pablo Marín is pitted generally reside in his own inadequacies. Further, by bringing in other protagonists of the same class and providing quick sketches of their problems, she gives a broad cross-section of middle-class life in Madrid during the 1950's. That she felt both techniques held validity is obvious, for in her next novel elements from *We Riveros* and *Public Servant* are combined to produce another original study.

CHAPTER 6

The Episodic Novel:
Relativity and Literary Technique

T HE next novel to appear, *El pez sigue flotando (The Fish Stays Afloat)*, was published three years after *Public Servant*.[1] In this work Miss Medio reintroduces Lena from *We Riveros* as one of the characters. Lena's perspicacious comments are clearly guideposts to orient the reader toward the general philosophy of the book.

Like *Public Servant*, the novel takes place in Madrid, but centers around an apartment house with its typical inner courtyard and expands its scope to include an even wider variety of characters than the preceding work. Short chapters take up one tenant after another in brief sketches of their lives, which Miss Medio begins, drops, and picks up later in random patterns. Each sketch is well drawn and designed to pique the reader's curiosity, often stopping abruptly at the point of greatest interest. Thus the author manipulates the strings of ten separate stories, with over twenty major and minor characters. The early transitions between consecutive chapters are simple references to the next person in question. For example, one character sees another out of the window and the story then moves on to the second character. Their proximity in the apartment house is the common denominator which allows the author to move easily, without excessive introductory material hampering the flow of the action.

I   The Fish Stays Afloat

There are two main stories in the novel, although they too are presented piecemeal. In the first, Mr. Morales, the owner of a small store, is fascinated by a charming woman who comes in to leave needlework that he sells on commission. He falls in love with her and, intrigued by the way she avoids talking about her life, creates a special image of her. Finally, he devotes his spare time to daydreaming about her. He is disillusioned to learn that she is Gina Planell, wife of a doctor, from the same apartment house. She has taken up knitting to have a little spending money because of the strict regulations imposed by her mother-in-law.

82

The actual details of Mr. Morales' story take second place to the sensitive exposition of a state of mind. The skill of the narrator is evident in her revelation of how loneliness makes him seize on this adventure, in the crescendo of his feelings, and his elation at finally discovering someone who can understand him. The absence of any erotic implication changes his fantasy relationship from the instinctual to the Platonic plane: his main desire is to have a home, with a loving companion. Morales is a lonely middle-aged man; he needs someone to share his life, and as much of his fantasy derives from a basic need of understanding and communication as from adolescent daydreams of an unknown woman.

The extended treatment of the situation allows the reader a sympathetic understanding for the character; deprived of a possible omniscience, the reader shares the same surprises and shock when the truth is known. Clearly Gina had planned no subterfuge; she had established a friendly business relationship and nothing more. Yet the impression remains that a fragile dream has shattered and that companionship and interdependence do not fare well in this world.

The second character of major importance is Marta Ribé, whose drama unfolds along opposite lines from Morales' need for love and companionship. Marta longs for independence—economic and emotional—and like Morales, she builds another, happier life on a possibility. Yet this independence carries with it the price of sacrificing another person and therefore her feelings are more ambivalent, for they involve love and guilt in equal measure. She is a poor typist who must work night and day to support herself and her old servant Tata, for whom she feels responsible. Marta must do the work at home because Tata is old and sick, and therefore her opportunities are limited and the pay small. Marta often thinks of what it would be like to be free and be able to get a better job away from the apartment. She is torn between affection for the old lady and her feeling of guilt at wishing to be independent. Tata has a bad heart attack, but recovers:

> Marta Ribé goes back to the bedroom. From the door she looks at Tata, who sleeps peacefully. The tenderness which the possible death of Tata revived in her, dissolves now in a protest: (You will have Tata for many years. . . . For many years. . . . For many years. . . . All that remain of my youth. To live alone, free . . ., free. Not to have to love anyone. . . . Because I love Tata. A lot. I love her a lot. If I didn't love her . . . I would leave her in the Home, of course, like she says . . . (pp. 133–34)

Finally, Tata has another attack, and as Marta fumbles with the syringe to give the necessary injection, her thoughts of saving the old woman alternate with the idea that this death would liberate her:

> Hurry up, Marta. The syringe is in the closet. And the box of ampoules. Don't hesitate. A minute can be decisive. Do you hear, Marta? Do you hear? Yes, Marta Ribé hears. But she thinks:
> 'If I wouldn't react, it would all be very simple. A few difficult minutes . . . Then, nothing . . . Then, yes, freedom! Freedom! A new life.' (p. 235)

The apparatus slips from her hand—accidentally or purposely?—and breaks. When she returns to the bedroom, she finds that Tata has already died.

Miss Medio emphasizes the oppressive heat in the cheap apartment, the necessity and feeling of obligation which bind her to the typewriter daily, and the sensation that Marta's prison is one of love, not hate. Tata's passive resignation, her devotion for the girl, are ties which bind much more than duty, for Tata feels useless and often suggests going to a home for old people. Thus the pangs of guilt enter into the relationship, as the young woman alternately realizes that Tata would be helpless without her, but also that, free of her, Marta could make something of her life. The complex emotional pattern is developed with great tact and understanding as Miss Medio suggests the changes through which Marta passes: annoyance, repentance, love, and the struggle between what duty demands (abnegation and unselfish giving) and the need for self-fulfillment (independence which can come only with Tata's death).

Thus neither of the two "main" characters—Marta and Morales—has satisfactorily fulfilled his desire. Marta, of course, sees her wish come true, but the price is too high for contentment. The two opposite movements toward a goal (one toward obligation; the other away from it) end in similar states of unhappiness and disillusionment, and this rather pessimistic tone sets the stage for the other lives which revolve around Marta and Morales. The author, however, generally refrains from comments which would color the work emotionally. She records rather like a camera and is subjective mainly in her selection and arrangement of episodes. The reader must judge for himself.

Around these more detailed stories, Dolores Medio draws shorter, episodic chapters concerning the lives of the other people in the apartment. Each has one special interest which the novelist develops:

José Cilleiro, the concierge, has his heart set on a transfer to a new apartment building where he will get a uniform and better tips, and is disappointed when the position is given to someone else. Vera Martínez, who makes her living dancing and getting clients to buy drinks in a dance hall, resisting their invitations to set her up, finally gives herself to a student who obviously has no money, but who can offer what she really needs: a sense of innocence and purity. Víctor Senosiain, who at first did not want children, becomes more and more excited at the prospect of a child, but is crushed when it is still-born at eight months. Madame Garín, the owner of a sewing school, thinks of all the unmarried men in the building who need love; she feels that she would be the perfect wife because of her tact and sympathy, yet she refuses to recognize these qualities in others when a fellow tenant, Dr. Brau, describes how another woman sacrificed her happiness in favor of his. Unable to resist the temptation, Juana Galán takes a lovely doll that a rich child has forgotten on a park bench; it is a luxury she cannot afford to give her little girl because they are very poor and hardly have enough to eat well. Above it all—literally and figuratively—is Lena Rivero, the novelist, who lives on the top floor and scandalizes the tenants by occasionally sliding down the bannisters. She is eyed suspiciously by the others, and some even make remarks about her incorporating their problems into her literature. But Lena also has her own adventure: her meeting, resistance, and final acceptance of the love offered to her by a sculptor she has met at a party. In her apartment she also has a toy aquarium with a plastic fish which always floats to the top of the water, no matter at what angle she turns the globe. From this symbolic possession comes the title of the novel.[2]

II   *The Episodic Novel*

In *The Fish Stays Afloat* Miss Medio has replaced the traditional single character with a myriad of secondary stories as background; each person has equal importance to the extent that his own narration replaces the previous one and continues a complementary line of development. The technique of presenting multiple characters is of structural significance, for the author deliberately fragments the usual linear arrangement of the novel, breaking off one to begin another, and not returning to the first until several chapters have passed. Using a wide lens which captures simultaneous action, she presents a *tranche de vie* which creates a greater illusion of reality, since the "observer" would in theory see these adventures episodically in real life.

There is, however, a marked effort to overcome the flat impression which the camera's impersonal eye could afford; the author only uses exterior, circumstantial reality as a springboard to enter wholly into the characters' inner world. After a brief introduction to the situation, the reader spends most of his time following the interior musings of the protagonists. Once introduced, the characters take over the task of exposition without the interference of the novelist, by means of interior monologues which aptly convey their situation. The rather disconnected and colloquial thought patterns of the concierge, for example, are reproduced with exactitude and a good dose of humor; as he goes to see about the possible new job, he notices that his fingernails are dirty:

("The heck with my nails! . . . No, if I . . . I . . .") He puts his hands in his pockets and promises himself to be very careful about not displaying them in front of Mr. Bofill.

("I can't do everything myself, I say. Clean this, clean that . . . . In the new place, cleaning women, of course . . . Cleaning house is woman's business. I'll be someone of consequence and can't . . .")

The annoyance of discovering he has dirty nails doesn't lessen the pleasure that he now experiences. It is a "visit." He has allowed himself to walk past the conciergerie, like a gentleman.

("St. Teresa said it. 'Keep your mind on your business.' And who was St. Teresa? Practically nobody . . . Heck . . . The greatest and most important saint in all of Spain. And St. Teresa said this . . . Well, I'm not sure. Damián Soler says that, and he reads a lot of priests and men who write things like that. The heck with priests! What those priests don't know . . .")
(pp. 150–51)

Miss Medio's interest in fragmentation, brief sketches of emotional moments instead of the extended plots, and the multiple characters rather than the single "hero," point to an interesting cross between the short story and the novel, reminiscent of procedures used in Camilo José Cela's pioneer work *La colmena (The Hive)*, 1951, a novel which was so innovational in technique that it prompted one critic to call it the most valuable and significant work published in Spain since the Civil War.[3] Luis Romero followed suit with his Nadal winner *La noria (The Waterwheel)*, 1952, and Cela himself returned to this successful form in later works like *Tobagán de hambrientos (Toboggan of Hungry People)*, 1962. This technique departs somewhat from the orthodox *tranche de vie* procedure of the naturalists. The truncation of sustained action, the switching from one theme or character to another, orchestrating effects, and underlining parallels in human nature imply a greater intervention of the artist in his selection and disposition of events. The episodic nature of the novel, in effect, provides an impression of simultaneity. This, in turn, gives a richer view of human experience. It consciously reflects the philosophy of interdependence or coincidence of humanity; linear time has been broken by the non-sequential ordering of events. Each piece of the novel has been carefully cut, as in a puzzle, and only when the last piece has been slipped into place does the reader enjoy the privilege of the complete overview.

Each of these episodic novels uses a fragmentary technique to impress similar final results on the reader. A sense of totality, emanating from the microcosmos on which the author focuses, lends itself to generalizations about human nature, suffering, alienation, and other modern themes which are efficiently expressed by the multiplication of characters, creating a fellowship of the anonymous. This novelistic technique had a philosophical parallel thirty years before in the theories of José Ortega y Gasset, in his doctrine concerning perspective : a philosophical relativity which reconciles divergent points of view. Perhaps the *Tema de nuestro tiempo (The Theme of our Time)*, 1923, best expresses this idea. According to Ortega, each point of view can encompass only a limited perspective, which in turn forms part of a whole reality: "Cosmic reality is such that it can only be seen under a determined perspective. Perspective is one of the components of reality. Far from being its deformation, it is its organization."[4] In effect, reality is relative, since truth is only partial for the individual. Ideally, absolute truth can be obtained by joining together each individual "truth" to make a rounded picture, without negating the validity of the individual. These are all themes which would attract Miss Medio, who prefers to work from the human angle, an approach which is another point of coincidence with Ortega. Her personal connections with the philosopher and his students were responsible for her introduction to his ideas; her literature has constantly shown evidence of an abiding interest in his theories.[5]

The Fish Stays Afloat—as well as the other novels which use the fragmentary technique—is the novelistic translation of Ortega's idea of relativity. Each character presents a partial view of life, and if that were not enough, each life is presented piecemeal. Having finished the novel, the reader can put together the impressions gleaned from the totality of elements and thus come to his own conclusion. It is also necessary for the reader to derive his own ideas of the truth about any one character, for Miss Medio presents the various points of view, but does not dictate a final judgment. The interweaving of individual experience, however, offers a privileged overview : mutual dependencies, the ironies of parallel experience, cause and effect, and the paradox of similarity within diversity, are clever literary implementations of Ortega's idea of absolute truth through "perspectivism." The common denominators seem to be deprivation (emotional or economic), disillusionment, and above all, isolation. The neighbors of the novel are joined only by their physical proximity: Instead of forming a certain solidarity because of their problems, they continue blindly on their same course, not thinking of communicating with one another except for the most superficial things.

The novel closes with the same character and scene with which it opened: Lena and her aquarium, but some time has passed and the characters have undergone their respective experiences. This deliberate recreation encloses its own comment on existence : life continues only slightly modified by circumstances.[6] The characters return to their basic behavioral patterns or sink into their old ways. José Cilleiro begins thinking about a new job despite his disappointment, Madame Garín continues being lonely, Senén Morales starts the cycle over again when he eyes Juana Galán.

III   *Similarity within Diversity*

So again it is middle-class characters who form the nucleus of her novel. Refining the form with which she experimented in *Public Servant,* Miss Medio offers a wide range of characters with a spate of problems, most of which have no resolution. Although their troubles may be of the emotional variety (like Marta's or Morales'), the majority of worries stem from the lack of money (another similarity with *Public Servant*), which in turn becomes a motivating power in the sketches. Even if this preoccupation does not have first place in the description, the author or another character will invariably make a remark about the subject's financial status, showing that this concern is foremost in their lives.

In general, work holds no attraction for the characters; it is simply a means to continue existing. At times, dreams of money offer them an escape outlet: José Cilleiro thinks night and day of his new job, whose new status and comfort are symbolized by the impressive uniform he will wear. In a similar situation, Senén Morales' fantasy centers around love, which he has not experienced, and Gina Planell offers him an escape from his drab existence. Like José, he suffers a similar disillusionment; like him he also has the ability to begin anew. José dreams of a job in still another apartment house; Senén Morales eyes Juana Galán, and we assume that she will be the next object of his fancy.

The desire and necessity to give or receive love is the second important factor in this work and deserves mention at this point because together with the concern for money it becomes a common denominator for several characters in *The Fish Stays Afloat*. No one is free of problems; the few who have money pursue the higher ideals of companionship or search for love. But most of the tenants have no time for this, and thus Marta's desperation arises not from dislike for Tata, but from the economic pressures of supporting two people on her meagre salary. The intense struggle to make a living takes first place in the lives of many of the characters—Bruno Jiménez or Juana Galán are well-drawn examples of the suffering born of lack of money.

The pain of loneliness and the need for companionship beset those who have enough material comfort to be spared the anguish of poverty. Parallel stories—never touching but deliberately treating aspects of the same problem—develop themes of solitude and non-communication. The prototype for this, of course, is Mr. Morales, and as his story unfolds, other facets of similar cases offer a fuller perspective from which to view the entire problem. Madame Garín's inquisitiveness concerning the unmarried men in the apartment is simply a cry of loneliness. Veva Martínez gratuitously gives herself to a young man because he shows an innocence that restores her own sense of self respect :

> In the boy's arms, Veva Martínez does not feel the anxiety—desire or repulsion—that other men produce in her. Perhaps because now she is dancing to dance, as she did in her home town. He is not going to insist that she drink. He's not going to ask anything of her. . . . And she feels . . . .

("Yes, that's it—like a bath of purity, of chastity . . . yes, of sweetness . . .") (p. 204)

Lena Rivero's interior struggle concerning the sculptor would also
fall into this category. Neither as pathetic nor as desperate as the
other apartment dwellers, she approaches the problem in a more
analytical manner, with none of the emotional overtones which are
often part of the other characters' presentation. In a dialogue with
herself about her decision to accept or reject the sculptor, she compares him to the two men whom she truly loved in her life, her
father and her brother. "She thinks that, in her way, she was in love
with El Aguilucho. Later with Ger. Later, she fell in love with all
the men who seemed like him in some way. Now this man . . . "
(p. 146). Thinking back on her life, Lena realizes that after adolescence,

life continually diminished her ideals, destroyed her ideals. devoured her
ideals. It left only her ego as the sole objective. An "I" that begins to mock
everything with gentle irony . . .
    Only in the case of "You-I" her egoism falters. It falters temporarily,
waiting to become the center of gravity again.
    Ah! Yes, of course . . . Sometimes, like this morning, the shell in which
Lena Rivero has wrapped herself breaks, and a rivulet of tenderness
escapes through the cracks [. . .] (p. 251)

The "breaking of the shell of selfishness" through love, solidarity,
or friendship seems to offer some hope in an otherwise bleak picture,
for it is the only way we forget ourselves to serve others with disinterest. This idea is reinforced in the last chapter, which concerns
Lena and ties together the disparate threads in the main idea. She
finds an injured cat and brings it to her apartment to help it and give
it a home. As she is attending to the animal, she thinks about her own
egoism and her defense mechanisms, and she feels the fish is judging
her: "('Yes, I know what you want to throw up to me. . . Well, am
I the only one guilty of this selfishness?')" (p. 251). She thinks of
throwing the aquarium out into the courtyard, but realizes that this
would do no good: "the aquarium would break, the little stones, the
coral, the seaweed would fall to the bottom. . . But the Fish would
keep on floating over everything. The Fish which would continue
looking at her from there, with his immobile round eye" (p. 252).
The Fish now becomes a symbol of a higher, omnipresent agent

which judges one's actions; the *immobile* eye suggests its constant vigilance. The necessity of helping others with no intention of gain may be the very abstruse "message" which the novel offers, but Miss Medio does not choose to overemphasize the implications. "Deserving" characters do not receive rewards; Morales does not win his love; the fate of Veva and Lena is left untold.

Only one character clearly breaks the circle: Veva Martínez actively rebels when she resists the temptation to become the mistress of one of the men she meets in the dance hall. She opts for idealism instead, by leaving with the penniless student, whose youth and purity symbolize what she unknowingly had been searching for all this time. Lena Rivero may also have profited by her experience, although the author does not clearly state this. Her justification of the moment of disinterest, however, parallels Veva Martínez' sudden realization.

The significance of the title of the novel is also ambiguous, for Miss Medio contrives deliberately several interwoven images around the central symbol of the plastic fish. One idea, already discussed, is the fish as judge; another is the fish as a symbol of determinism, for the characters are never completely in control of their lives. This theme is suggested, but not developed to the extent of *Tomorrow, We Riveros,* or even *Public Servant:* "The patio is like an aquarium. When it remains in silence, the materials 'have sedimented.' And only the fish keeps on floating. The fish. Who is the fish? Where is the fish? ('Well, yes, here, in my aquarium. But he could also be that unknown factor that floats among men, without being seen. What governs them and makes them act, although they think they are acting freely.')" (p. 10). This quotation, from the first pages of the novel, suggests a guideline for the reader to follow. There is ample proof of man's dependence on circumstances: the unexpected pregnancy and miscarriage in the Senosiain household; Lena's acquaintance with the sculptor; Tata's death. Emotional or material deprivation may provide the opportune moment for a sudden, desperate change in personality (Morales or Juana Galán).

Still another interpretation is possible, based on the words "stays afloat" in the title. The idea of continuity could doubtless be an analogue with the life of the tenants: No matter what happens, the fish will float to the top of the aquarium; no matter what disappointments the people suffer, they must continue to live. The affirmation is for life and its continuance, but this is not an affirmation recognized as a positive good by the characters, but rather a law of nature which cannot be broken.

The Fish Stays Afloat has not received the critical attention it deserves, probably because it does not easily lend itself to analysis. It is, however, important in the total production of Miss Medio because of the continuing themes and character types (her use of the main character who is a woman and is intimately connected with Miss Medio's own experiences), and because of the technique which shows the deliberate effort to fuse form and content to expose her own philosophy of life.

IV   *Continuing Preoccupations*

The impact on the reader of *The Fish Stays Afloat* depends on an innovational technique which underscores the work's basic philosophical concerns. The themes show a renewed interest in basic subjects and character types which are indicative of Miss Medio's continuing attention to certain aspects of society.

The numerous characters combine traits from all of the former works. Lena, naturally, recalls her younger version in *We Riveros*; as in the first novel, she maintains a certain distance from her fellow tenants, with a resultant objectivity which permits her to be spokesman for the author. The other characters also derive their personalities from prototypes eastablished earlier. They are people from the middle or lower class, and like their models, are beset with problems: economic preoccupations, the hardships of the sublessee, noncommunication and solitude are constants in every work. Even more outstanding is a common pattern which the majority of these characters follow. They forge themselves a hope based on a rather loose interpretation of possibility in their lives : they may create an ideal person (Morales' idea of Gina is entirely imaginary, much in the same way as Pablo Marín's Natalia); they may long for an improvement in present conditions (physical or emotional). In none of these cases does the ideal materialize : on the contrary, Miss Medio deliberately pricks the dream bubble at its height. In *Public Servant,* Natalia is unreal; Pablo loses his chance at the lottery and his wife. *The Fish. . .* also elaborates stories of failure: Gina turns out to be married; José Cilleiro does not get his job; a miscarriage terminates Senosiain's plans for his son. From the distance between reality and ideal arises the pathos notable in the short stories, but the deliberate lack of emphasis on any one character diffuses concentrated empathy, making the reader aware of parallels in life, of many small misfortunes rather than a single great tragedy. Miss Medio has striven to communicate this idea in the earlier works; in *The Fish Stays Afloat* the unique literary formula has provided a successful means for developing her continuing preoccupations.

CHAPTER 7

Teaching Experiences: Reality and Fiction

A second alter ego of Dolores Medio, Irene Gal, is the heroine of *Diario de una maestra (Diary of a Schoolteacher)*, published two years after *The Fish Stays Afloat.*[1] In accordance with the novelist's theory of reality as the basis for literature, we know that much of this novel reflects portions of her life; specifically, her experiences in Nava, a small town near Oviedo, where she taught briefly until she was removed from her post because of her "revolutionary methods."[2]

The title of this work would lead one to expect a first-person, day-by-day account of the life of a schoolteacher, but the author actually uses the third-person narrative for the majority of the work. She gives the impression of a diary by dating the chapters and describing thoughts so intimate that they would only be revealed through this kind of instrument. The novel is composed of two parts, which, like *Public Servant,* use two aspects of a single person as a point of departure. Through Irene Gal, the teacher, Dolores Medio describes her work as a rural teacher, and by extension, airs her own views on education. Irene's affair with her teacher, Máximo Saenz, brings out the "other" Irene: the character as a woman and a human being.

I Diary of a Schoolteacher

Irene is sent to teach in La Estrada after studying at the University of Oviedo. Her innovational methods are met with suspicion by the townspeople, whose opposing factions of liberals and conservatives agree only in their distrust of the new teacher and her methods. She tries to introduce modern ideas in her school; instead of the traditional methodology, she builds her lessons on a single theme, using the interest of the students as a guide rather than a preset lesson plan. One of her greatest *coups* is winning over sixteen-year-old Timoteo, the town reprobate. She uses psychology and good will and soon has a staunch ally in him. Timoteo becomes for Irene a symbol of the town itself, which she hopes to educate to the new ways, and slowly she wins the people's confidence. Irene's new methods soon take effect; she has the children gardening, working with animals, and learning practical material that will be useful to them in later life.

She is in Oviedo when the Civil War breaks out. Máximo has disappeared, and Irene finally discovers him in jail in a remote village. However, her stay there is short-lived; a childhood friend, now a Falangist, forces her to return to Oviedo, because he wants to protect her from the radical elements. The war evokes many comments on human nature and man's relationship to man. Irene's first reaction is anger because of her involvement in something beyond her control: "('It's injust, it's . . . yes, it's criminal. Why does youth have to pay for the disastrous politics of the older generation?')" (p. 116). Within the philosophizing about war and man is one of the recurrent ideas, first expressed by Máximo Saenz: the doctrine of love and good will as the only way to peace. "(Máximo was right. There is no good will among men. When it would be so easy to love one another . . . to help one another. It's easy to be good. It's sufficient to have good will . . . "Peace on Earth to men of good will" . . . But there is no good will among men. Men do not want Peace')" (p. 113). The dependence on love had been mentioned earlier—the epigraph of the novel comes from St. John of the Cross: "Where you do not find love, give love and you will encounter love." Irene puts this idea into practice throughout the work : first, a little effort at love and understanding on Irene's part gains Timoteo's friendship. Her openness and affection next win the students, and then the townspeople. If this theory proves successful on an individual level, Irene believes that it is viable on a wider scale. Perhaps the same kind of understanding and effort could have averted a national disaster.

Working in a Nationalist hospital also crystallizes Irene's feelings about helping her fellowman, and allows her to put her motto into practice. She works in a ward for wounded Moroccans. These "Moors" are dirty, and most women prefer the Officers' ward: "But the Moors are also men . . . wounded men . . . Humanity . . . Fronts, jails, hospitals . . . Humanity, poor humanity!" (p. 119).

When she can return to the town, she learns that Timoteo has died defending the priest, once his bitter enemy. Irene is soon released from her job because of her liberal affiliations. It is impossible to get employment without references, and even the factories will not hire her because of her connections. She finally decides that domestic service is the only answer, since she needs the money to live and to support Máximo, who never learns that she has lost her position as schoolteacher.

Miss Medio skips over Irene's life until 1943, at which time Irene returns to La Estrada to pick up where she left off. The war is over, but everyone has suffered its effects in some way. The townspeople receive her warmly, and allow her to teach as she wants, but there are still human problems to be solved, and Irene continues to use love as the basis for her philosophy of life : she encourages an illegitimate child, helps the unhappy woman who caused Timoteo's death to comes to terms with herself, comforts and entertains the old. She remains faithful to Máximo, who has been in jail for eight years, even when her love is questioned by a would-be suitor.

She divides her life between helping the children and the people of the village and waiting for Max, who, she learns, is soon to be released from jail. Irene happily makes plans for his imminent arrival: she obtains a job for him in the village to give him a chance to readjust before he returns to his intellectual pursuits. Her excitement soon turns to despair: Max tells her that he plans to leave again that very day. In effect, Máximo not only denies their love but the principles and ideals he himself had instilled in her:

> Humanity! We are humanity, Irene Gal . . . Each one of us, with our private lives and our problems. We, who are made of flesh and bone, and not words and more words on paper! And who cares about our problems? No one but ourselves! . . . And we have a right to be happy . . . and to live peacefully. As for me, I have decided to live my life without paying attention to other people's problems. (p. 223)

Max is a broken man, disillusioned by his years in prison. He realizes the death of their love even before Irene senses the reason for his arrival: "Now, the twenty years which separate them have widened like a ditch . . . In the ditch . . . there is also a heap of corpses. Corpses of ideals. Perhaps only of *points of view*" (p. 221). [Miss Medio's italics].

After Max's abrupt termination of their affair, Irene believes that her life no longer holds any meaning. She wanders into the countryside, intending to commit suicide. As she approaches the edge of a cliff and is about to step forward, the voice of "Monkey Face," a little paralytic she has been helping, stops her. Irene turns and sees the child working her way toward her on crutches: "For a few minutes, Irene Gal looks at her without understanding. "Monkey

Face" was outside her thought, her life, forming part of a world which she had forgotten. And now that world is coming to seek her, to reclaim her in order to place her again in the center of it. In the place which belongs to her" (p. 232). Thus Irene acknowledges the primacy of life and duty, which she places above her personal loss, and returns to the village where she will help others.

II   *Women Characters in Dolores Medio's Works*

The primary focus of *Diary* . . . emphasizes the strengthening of Irene's character and the manner in which her adventures affect, change, or modify her existence. Since the main concentration will be on the characters, it follows that the creation of the town, the atmosphere, and the historical moment take second place to the examination of Irene Gal, woman and teacher. Her development is clearly mapped out, for Dolores Medio makes sure that the reader follows the maturation process the character undergoes. To this end, the author studies the effects of environment on personality, showing through reactions to specific situations how basic character is modified only slightly (her idealism is never tarnished, her sense of duty remains foremost) because she is a strong person. To the possibilities offered to her, Irene applies her motto of love, with the resultant lesson that duty and unselfish interest often must precede personal desires. Her strength of character allows her to follow her motto and provides a reason to live; the contrast is Max, whose experiences overwhelm him and finally force him to change.

The novelist has excelled in painting women characters. This is not to say that she does not understand male psychology; *Public Servant,* for example, is an excellent portrait of a man. But there is no doubt that her preference is for feminine psychology, perhaps again because of an identification with the character or character traits. We may assume that much of the novelist herself has been put into her female protagonists, and although not all the adventures spring directly from her own life to the novel, they offer partial insights into experiences in Miss Medio's life, and especially much of her own opinions, as well as experiences that would fall into her "realm of possibility" (see p. 28 above).

Lena Rivero, in Miss Medio's first novel, several characters in *The Fish Stays Afloat,* including Lena herself, and now Irene in *Diary of a Schoolteacher* also seem to share traits in common: they have a strong sense of duty, a moral and ethical streak born of an idealism which makes them dreamers, yet the common sense to put their ideas into practice. They have a sense of humor, no visible family ties, are independent, are given to rambling soliloquies on life and the state of man. Irene and the older Lena have lovers; once they decide to take one, they give themselves completely with no regrets. It is this insistence on total sacrifice—whether to a man *(Diary . . . , Fish . . .)* or a cause or ideal (all three novels), that creates a sisterhood among the characters. They are decisive, compassionate, strong-willed, yet giving; intelligent yet ingenuous, antithetical characteristics which give them depth and bring them to life for the reader.

The females are also endowed with a wider and more comprehensive view of life then the males. They tend to philosophize about life, but they seem to be able to grasp immediately the essentials of the situation, to act without pretext, to be basically honest with themselves and others—no matter what the cost—and to preserve within themselves a vestige of innocence, ingenuity, and even naïvete that remains from their childhood. This is especially true in *Diary . . . ,* in which the author repeatedly uses adjectives that refer to Irene's childlike aspects : words and phrases like "almost a child," "childlike eyes," "childlike look," "ingenuousness," describe Irene. Even with the other women, the author points out the same characteristics : Lena Rivero still retains a youthful innocence despite her new maturity (see p. 45 above); even words like "childish happiness" or the fact that the older Lena likes to slide down the banisters also create a special artlessness.

The novels and several short stories use women to explore aspects of society: its pressures, restrictions, or the necessity for change. She investigates their relationship with the social whole (in rebellion against the position into which the characters are forced, in conflict with traditional ideas which they wish to change), with other individuals (their intimate life and love or the lack of it; the wider scope in their relationship with others), and finally face to face with themselves, in their frank self-questioning and autoanalysis.

Each woman is shown in her relationship with a man (there is a clear trajectory from the nebulous figure of the Prince of Asturias and the miner in *We Riveros* to the concrete presence of Max in *Diary . . .*), which generally presents some kind of problem which must be resolved in the final acceptance or rejection of the man;

each evolves a definite philosophy concerning life (generally embracing ethical priciples); and each illuminates another aspect of the problem which women face in the world outside their home. Thus there is a natural continuity in the exploration of woman's role in society throughout Miss Medio's work. *We Riveros* showed concern for the status of women and a protest against the traditional role assigned to them. *The Fish Stays Afloat* presents several women who strive for independence by trying to earn their own way in life, or by attempting to define their role in society. *Diary of a Schoolteacher* would obviously have occasions which permit the discussions of Miss Medio's theories on women. In this novel, the war precipitates the natural evolution of women toward independence: "An avalanche of women have rushed to conquer the positions which the men abandon to go to the front, Irene among them . . . Woman begins to enjoy the right and the pleasure of her economic independence and now an opportunity to get it is at hand" (p. 143).

The preoccupation with rights and privileges is not exclusive to women. The author is also interested in humanity as a whole, and her sympathy and compassion for the characters—whether good or bad—easily prove this. Irene's many efforts to help the town and educate the children is the practical application of the theory; her discussions with Máximo present this concern on a more theoretical level. Good education, democracy, the political future, social evolution, and equality are topics which reveal the early idealism of both characters.

III   *Secondary Characters*

If Dolores Medio's women tend to follow a pattern, the men in these works do also : they are generally weak and subordinate to or dependent on their female companions. The male characters in *We Riveros* are too few to generalize about—the only important one is Ger, and he obviously an exception to the rule. The main character in *Public Servant* is a weak man, indecisive, dependent on his wife for the only affection he can get; dependent on a dream woman for his hopes. *The Fish Stays Afloat* offers a wider panorama of males (although the female element is still dominant), but they still have secondary roles or are generally irresolute, like Morales, the shopkeeper who searches for love, or they remain in the background, like Gina's husband. Máximo Saenz, Timoteo, and Timoteo's grandfather are background characters in *Diary of a Schoolteacher,* and depend on Irene for strength, love, understanding, or comfort.

The character development of the men in *Diary of a Schoolteacher* reveals interesting changes in the course of the work. Each person is put to the test in some way, the Civil War being one of the major trials, although there are other less important events. Max's idealistic feelings about humanity, first expounded in his lectures at the beginning of the work, serve to define his personality: a moral, ethical man whose theories sound very good in the abstract. His leadership and supposed strength of character attract Irene at once, and she turns him into an ideal man with heroic proportions greatly magnified by the enforced separation (much in the same way as Pablo Marín conceived of Natalia Blay). Max is thus established as the leader and dominant figure of the couple. Irene's thoughts about him place their relationship in the father-daughter or teacher-pupil category:

> When she is with Máximo Saenz—a trick of the subconscious?—she gives herself over to him in such a way that it even makes her tired to think. She is overcome by a type of lassitude, of letting herself go . . . She not only gives him a material surrender, but also an intellectual one. . . She likes to abandon her personality, to feel like a child, to live and act like a child who knows she is spoiled and protected. (p.85)

Irene's work, in which unselfish interest has conditioned her, molds her character and prepares her for the reversal of roles necessary in the second part: She becomes the strong person, a symbolic indication of her new maturity.

Several critics have censured Miss Medio for Max's abrupt change of character, signaling it as the major weakness in the work. Juan Luis Alborg, for example, states: "The political decline of the man is, in my judgment, quite inconsistent, and I am inclined to think that it is a question of a forced solution that the writer has had to adopt, perhaps to give viability to the novel. . . . If she had the man persist in his ideas and his love, it would be necessary for the couple to maintain their position of rebellion for which they had fought and suffered; but then her novel would touch on very difficult political points. . . . It was necessary, then to 'get rid of' the character, not only in his love for the heroine, but also for his moral posture (since it was impossible, as we can see, to disentangle both aspects), so that then, empty and contemptible, he could be impeached, while the protagonist remained in a poetic and resigned renunciation, bathed in sweet pessimism."[3]

Miss Medio has answered the charge of inconsistency of character by stating that Max comes directly from an important episode in her own life. Commenting on the verisimilitude of this character, she states,

> Of course I knew Max! I knew him so well that he is the most authentic character in my whole work. I have been criticized by the left wing because of the fate of this character, but *it was the authentic one* [Miss Medio's italics]. He was a fabulous man, but jail, and life, destroyed him. This is very human, although it may not be to the liking of a certain group. We must not falsify things in a novel, even though they hurt our political, and even personal, ideas. The respect for the character must come before other interests. At least, this is my motto.[4]

Since Miss Medio does not develop Max to the same extent as Irene, it is a surprise to the unprepared reader to see his complete volte-face at the end of the work. There are, however, possible reasons for the seemingly unexplained change. First, the major character in the work is Irene; the author has followed her development slowly, injecting anecdotes as signposts along the trajectory of her growth. Max's function is to help Irene form her own philosophy and serve as an intermediate step to independence. His personal life and formative experiences are not made available to the reader; his personality is fully formed at the beginning of the work; his maturity and set ideas exercise a decisive influence on Irene's life.

Furthermore, Miss Medio constantly employs a technique in her novels which places the reader on the level of the character by withdrawing from her place as omniscient narrator. The suddenness of his change, the unexplained defection may puzzle the reader, but he is made to receive the same impression as Irene. The author forces him to view the situation from Irene's perspective, thus making her reactions more immediate. In Max, Irene has created an ideal person who incarnates the abstract principles she holds most dear. She and Max spend long hours discussing these principles, but she is the one who puts them into practice. His sudden about-face may not be a radical change in character, but the necessary confrontation of the ideal with its true counterpart: the real Max, which Irene can see only after she has matured, can never equal the one she has created in her own mind.

More minor characters are developed in brief vignettes which reveal the rather unhappy condition of men. They serve as examples of Irene's ability to help the townspeople and thus are generally more pathetic than usual, since they have certain problems. Timoteo's grandfather is painted with great sympathy as an old man whose need for affection makes him gravitate toward the understanding schoolteacher. It becomes a ritual for her to straighten his scarf and kiss him on the cheek, a ceremony which the old man looks forward to as the bright spot in his day. "She-wolf"—the woman responsible for Timoteo's death—is another example of this novelist's presentation. Miss Medio describes her as an unhappy woman, driven to this extreme act because of grief for her son, killed years ago.

In his analysis of the work, A. Valencia states that the novel's major defect is in the ideation and development of the minor characters, whose function is too subordinate to that of Irene and who are often inconsistent. Max's breakdown, for example, seems gratuitous because he was not developed enough. He continues: "They live less for themselves than in order to justify the dominant route of the protagonist, to whom they supply 'tests' of emotions, conduct, and events."[5]

In effect, each of the characters does supply some new test of Irene's character, offers some new fire in which to temper the resistance of her personality. Miss Medio has created them to enhance Irene's point of view and their major purpose is to be subordinate to her, but this is not necessarily a defect in technique. They live in spite of this role, for the novelist has shown herself successful in creating the short sketch, the character who can come to life in one episode, stand out through a single interesting or pathetic trait, and then naturally recede into the background. All these figures form a living mobile around Irene, who acts as the catalyst in their lives— helping, loving, molding, rejoicing, or grieving with them. The sketches of these people enrich the background of daily living which the novelist feels is so important. This is still another manifestation of the *pequeño vivir*—the everyday life of the ordinary person— which Miss Medio feels is the basis of history itself.

IV   *From Theory to Practice*

Irene, the woman, is studied amply in her love for Max and her relationship with the individuals in the town. Irene, the educator, is developed with special attention, for she is to reflect theories that form the core of Dolores Medio's philosophy of life. The author has had a lifelong connection with education : the private classes she gave as a girl, her summer job as governess, full-time teaching at Nava, classes given during her stay in Madrid are the practical manifestation of her interest. Beyond teaching as a career, however, Miss Medio has always professed a great concern for more theoretical aspects of education, ranging from classroom methodology to instruction through mass media (e.g., her theory of using literature to raise the cultural level of the country).

The education and psychology of the child would naturally interest a dedicated teacher, but Dolores Medio the writer has also made an effort to point out the educational benefits in art. She uses the novel as an opportunity for instructional means, and inserted into a fictional framework are the ideas she has discussed in her theoretical works. A series of articles written around the decade of *Diary* . . . reveal that she considers that art serves the double function of entertainment and instructional tool. One article equates phases in a child's development with the type of story which most interests him;[6] an extensive series deals with children's literature;[7] another series treats children's movies and the problem of juvenile delinquency, pointing out the educational values which the cinema could easily supply.[8] Further articles give practical advice using psychology to answer questions: in "Benavente and Education," she states, "If the old proverb [. . .] 'Call a man a thief and he will steal,' offers a lesson, although a negative one, the opposite, 'Trust in the man and he will respond to your trust,' could well become a pedagogical maxim."[9] In *Diary of a Schoolteacher,* this is the principle that Irene applies to Timoteo. She buys a chicken for the school, but lets Timoteo think that they stole it together. She then makes him understand that even petty thievery is wrong, and through her own pretended guilt feelings, makes him respect the property rights of others. Still another piece, written with a sense of humor and a keen understanding of and sympathy for children, suggests that although we should let our children have the privilege of dreaming as long as possible, we should not allow them to get mistaken notions about reality.[10] The material in these articles reveals the same kind of outlook which Irene showed in teaching the children in her charge. Rather than learning for the sake of learning, both author and protagonist suggest that every opportunity should be seized to demonstrate how one should live ethically and morally.

The place that is accorded to education in Miss Medio's scale of values may be seen in her comments about the state of teaching after the Civil War. The religious vocabulary which she uses communicates the awe in which she holds it and the "blasphemy" of those who have broken what she considers to be a sacred trust:

> She cannot think, without deep grief, about the false position in which some unscrupulous educators have put themselves: by paying homage to their political ideas—very respectable ideas in other contexts—they dared to profane the sacred enclosure of a school, on whose altar only the incense of Peace and Love for humanity may be burned. They imposed their sympathies toward a determined sector of the nations at war on the children and on the entire population [. . .] (pp. 155–56).

In *Diary of a Schoolteacher,* Miss Medio has illustrated her theories of education; these are transmitted in the description of the new methods and in comments on the state of education in Spain; the reader has the opportunity to see the plan introduced to the town. Since she has always preferred to present her case slowly and clearly, with many examples, *Diary* . . . offers a lively, interesting account of the abstract idea, liberally sprinkled with anecdotes attesting to the validity of the method. Only rarely does she express herself in generalities, but these, too, always have practical social implications. For example, she poses the necessity for mixing children of all economic backgrounds: "One day, not very far off, it will seem absurd that there were schools for rich people and schools for poor ones . . . As absurd and immoral as slavery seems to us today. Education should be the same for all, with no other difference than that of the intellectual capacity of the student" (p. 56).

On the instructional level, her enthusiasm for a change in methodology stems from her own experiences as a teacher. One critic describes the state of conditions at that time and how changes in education were received: "It is important to take into account the years in which the action takes place, which are the ones which immediately precede our Civil War. In those days the new educational currents, inspired by ideals of renewal and liberty, tried to break through old routines; and any innovation of this type (many of them later became 'normal' methods, questioned by no one) acquired at that moment the character of a rebellious undertaking, nonconformist and heterodox, vis-à-vis the petrified norms which were considered perfect. Any reform generally suggested that its defenders were connected with some kind of radical position. Any suggestion of the slightest change, criticism or improvement—successful or not—always smacked [. . .] of leftist positions."[11]

These "radical methods of change" described by Juan Luis Alborg were practiced by Miss Medio before her dismissal. She followed the tenets of the Dalton School Plan, an experimental system which Miss Helen Parkhurst introduced in England and the United States (in Dalton, Massachusetts, hence the name). Influenced by the Montessori method, Miss Parkhurst's idea was to keep the individual student in mind, providing opportunities for the slow as well as the bright child. The word laboratory is the key here, and actually refers to the room in which a single subject is taught. The basic principles of the Dalton Laboratory Plan are: (1) freedom to pursue individual interests; and (2) cooperation or the interaction of group life. The student determines his own rate of speed, since there are no formal classes with set hours. In Miss Parkhurst's own words, "Briefly summarized, the aim of the Dalton Plan is a synthetic aim. It suggests a simple and economic way by means of which a school as a whole can function as a community. The conditions under which the pupils live and work are the chief factors of their environment, and a favorable environment is one which provides opportunities for spiritual as well as mental growth. It is the social experience accompanying the tasks, not the tasks themselves which stimulates and furthers both these kinds of growth. Thus the Dalton Plan lays emphasis upon the importance of the child's living while he does his work, and the manner in which he acts as a member of society, rather than upon the subjects of his curriculum. It is the sum total of these twin experiences which determine his character and his knowledge."[12]

This plan obviously fits into Miss Medio's interest in the individual rather than the idea, and its combination of personal and social needs recalls passages from *Public Servant* as well as *Diary of a Schoolteacher*, providing an interesting point of reference when we consider the author's opinions on the effect of environment on character. *Diary of a Schoolteacher* is the Dalton Plan put into literary practice. Máximo Saenz refers to it in his first lecture as part of the new philosophy of education. Irene then uses the Plan in her reorganization of the country school : the children are allowed to work on projects that interest them; they work separately as well as in groups. Irene's success is apparent in the cooperation and love of the children and final respect of the townspeople.

V   *Philosophy and Ethics*

The novelist returns to her favorite philosopher, Ortega y Gasset, in this work. His doctrine of relativity, first implemented in *The Fish Stays Afloat*, although never acknowledged as such, reappears as a leitmotif which quite naturally emphasizes the theory behind her idea of human tolerance and comprehension. Here, Miss Medio becomes much more explicit in voicing the doctrine of "partial view": Irene as a child was puzzled when an art teacher praised entirely different drawings of the same object, saying that each was an exact reproduction of the same model. "Thus the first lesson in perspective was also the first lesson in philosophy for Irene Gal. She thought: possibly there does exist an absolute truth, a truth interpreted by our senses, a subjective truth. Then it is absurd and pretentious to believe that we, and only we, are right when we express our *point of view*" (pp. 48–49). [Miss Medio's italics].

Thinking of this, then, permits us to be more tolerant of our fellowman, since he also has his own partial truth seen from his own angle:

> Irene Gal cannot say when she began to accept this business of the relative right of each one, but she does know that this observation made her extremely understanding and tolerant of the *point of view* of the other person. In each case she says to herself: "He sees it this way from the social stratum in which he is situated. From his profession. Because of his age. Or his sex. Or simply, interpreted from a determined mentality. . . . In order to convince him of my truth, I would have to place him on my own plane. But would it be more just, more sensible, to put myself in his place?" (p. 49)

This theory, of course, provides a fitting accompaniment to Irene's profession of love and understanding. One can easily apply the philosophy of point of view to the opposing sides during the Civil War by considering them as persons rather than as ideas, and understanding that each individual views life from a different perspective. This is what prompts Irene to work in a Nationalist hospital, although she ostensibly was a liberal. When she returns to school, she sees the practical application of this: "On the benches of the school the sons of the fallen on both fronts, the sons of the executed men from the two sides were to sit together. For each child, his father is a hero. His cause, the good cause. His grief, just . . . "(p. 123)

The culmination of this principle is in the doctrine of forgiveness, which is no more than an extension of human understanding and

sympathy. When Irene meets the woman who caused Timoteo's
death, her anger and disgust soon turn into pity. "The instinctive
disgust which Irene Gal feels toward 'She-wolf' begins to dissolve
in a feeling of pity, which leads her to find a justification for her
crimes:
('We all commit some crime. Sometimes we actually do it. The
occasion, the circumstances . . . Other times it is only wished for,
it is committed within us and human justice cannot ask us to account
for it [. . .]')" (p. 167). Thus, by putting herself in the woman's
position, she can understand her and forgive her. More than that,
she wants to help her, and applying the same kind of psychology
she used on the woman's victim, she confides in her and tries to
bring her inner peace: " . . . Irene Gal decides not to leave without
speaking with 'She-wolf.' Without leaving a little peace, a little love
in her conscience, something, in short, which could serve as ferment
for a possible settling of accounts with herself, which is what really
matters." (p. 169)

Although *Diary of a Schoolteacher* is not a thesis novel in the
strict sense of the word, Miss Medio does leave an understated
message at the end of the book. She has prepared the reader for it by
an extended metaphor throughout the work; when reading a story to
the students, Irene tells about a boatman and a young boy who
wanted to cross the river. The boatman was old and insisted the
other help row; when the boy took hold of the oars, he found he
could not let them go. Miss Medio then applies the meaning of the
tale to Irene's life as the teacher thinks: " 'Well . . . Isn't something
like this happening to me? I tried to cross the river, only cross the
river and . . . '

Yes. It is clear. The Boatman who put the oars in her hand, does
not permit her to let them go yet" (pp. 82-83).

There are fleeting references to the story in later pages, but Miss
Medio uses it to the fullest advantage at the end of the work. As
Irene realizes that she must return to the town to help the people,
she smiles and says, " . . . the oars! The oars again . . . The Great
Boatman won't permit me to let them go" (p. 232). In view of her
ideas on the novel as one tool for education, it is obvious that Miss
Medio wishes the reader to assume that this tale does not refer exclusively to Irene's situation. Each of us has some moral or ethical
responsibility which he must fulfill, and he cannot let his personal
feelings interfere with his duty. For this reason Irene returns to the

village, although still suffering from her unhappy love affair. And, by analogy, Miss Medio reminds us of one's obligation to society, for one must give of himself and help others.

Diary . . . is the closest Miss Medio has come to a commentary on unsatisfactory conditions in Spain. As such, there are some affinities with the attitudes of the Generation of 1898—specifically Baroja—in pointing out the backwardness of the people, typified in their reactions to Irene's new methods. Distrust, suspicion, and resistance to any new idea characterize the town's attitude at first, and Irene makes a comment that could apply to the whole country as well as the microcosmic La Estrada: "The psychology of one people is no different from that of another. And people always receive every innovation, any effort at rebellion with distrust. And there are also politics, petty politics, which have turned each town, each village, each family into a wasp's nest" (p. 72). Yet this generalization can only be based on the specifically human situations in Dolores Medio's novels.

CHAPTER 8

The Individual and the Group: Patterns of Social Behavior

I N 1963 Miss Medio published *Bibiana*, the first novel in her
trilogy *Los que vamos de pie* (*We Who Go by Foot*).[1] The first-
person plural subject in the collective title is a device to establish
her own position with regard to the subject matter in the work:
she identifies herself with the class and the milieu she is describing,
creating a sympathetic bond, despite the implicit criticism which
the book offers.

I Bibiana

Bibiana is the wife of Marcelo Prats and mother of five children:
José, Xenius, Manuel, Natalia, and Francisca. These people, plus
a boarder, Massó, constitute her entire sphere of interest. Natalia,
the oldest child, is extremely independent, cool, with an undisguised
feeling of detachment from the family, of which she seems slightly
ashamed. From all signs, "Nat" is having an affair with a man of
some means, but there is no way to verify this. She wears a ring which
she insists is costume jewelry, but which seems to contain a precious
stone. Bibiana is terribly awed by her beautiful but surly child, and
can only surmise, but never ask, since Nat generally rejects Bibiana's
attempts to draw her out.

Certain episodes directly reveal just how concerned Bibiana is
about Nat. She realizes that her daughter had not menstruated for
several months and believes that she may be pregnant. When evidence proves to the contrary, Bibiana is so relieved that she goes
into her daughter's room, cries, and finally confesses the reason for
her happiness. Nat, however, is not given to the kind of woman-to-
woman confidences that Bibiana would so enjoy, and never really
clarifies the question. Her reply is, "Control your imagination a
little, mother, and don't dramatize . . . Do you think that a modern
woman lets herself fall just like that . . . . As for me, don't worry
that I'll make you a grandmother. Do you think I'm crazy?"
(p. 117). These words make Bibiana more unhappy and suspicious

than ever, for the simplicity of the words reveals more than Nat wished: "Bibiana Prats, overwhelmed with the weight of a new suspicion, remains seated on the chair in Nat's room with her hands crossed over her stomach" (p. 118).

Yet one of Bibiana's most outstanding qualities is her protectiveness toward her children, and even though her suspicions are strong, she refuses to take anyone into her confidence. Thus she keeps her doubts about Nat from her husband to avoid possible conflict and trouble; she may also feel that not voicing her thoughts may somehow avert misfortune. Her protectiveness appears with the other "problem" child, Xenius. The boy left school in Barcelona under mysterious circumstances that the parents were never able to verify. His propensity toward poetry has only increased Marcelo's suspicions that Xenius is a homosexual. When he tells Bibiana this, she bursts into tears, accusing her husband of not understanding and of hating his son. After recovering her self-control, she immediately tries to smooth things over by saying that there is no evidence for such accusations. Neither problem is resolved, and the reader is left in doubt as to the truth concerning Nat and Xenius.

The other children also present problems, but to a lesser degree. Francisca wants to leave school and become a beautician. Bibiana devises an elaborate plan to protect her from Marcelo's anger, but he acquiesces without arguing. She raises a barrier between her husband and the children, and does not insist that they face their own problems. There is one episode, however, in which Marcelo insists that Manuel, the youngest, go out and fight the street bully who has terrorized him. For once Bibiana sides with her husband in a dramatic scene in which the boy does not want to leave. Finally Manuel gets up his courage, and a bloody battle ensues in which neither wins, but from which Manuel emerges with a new evaluation of his own abilities.

Marcelo is rather gruff and hardworking; it seems that Bibiana has made an image of his innate ferocity that he does not deserve. He is most concerned about the children's ability to cope with life: how they are to react to it, how they will ádjust to it. He is keenly aware of the family's unstable economic position and of how his children are to fit into society; he voices strong opinions about certain unfavorable social conditions.

There are several hints that Marcelo may be seeing another woman. Once Bibiana finds lipstick on his handkerchief, but

Marcelo makes a joke of it. Bibiana thinks, "He says 'bah, bah' and talks a lot . . . But the handkerchief . . . I wonder if there is some sly woman who's getting his money. Old fool! A sly woman . . . Bibiana Prats corrects herself ('One shouldn't judge anyone . . . A woman has children and who's to blame! Who knows . . . The best person makes a slip. . . .')" (p. 166). The subject comes up again, but Bibiana does not choose to pursue it, nor does she act the silent martyr. Although she depends on Marcelo, she treats him rather as she treats the children. Apparently there are some things she would rather not know about and refuses to investigate further (perhaps a parallel with the position she takes concerning Nat's private life). In effect, her opinion of Marcelo can be summarized by the thoughts she has of him at the beginning of the novel: "(The same as the children . . . Marcelo is like a child . . . Good Lord, like a child . . . A child who's almost old, but a child, like the others, who needs her care just the way they do)" (pp. 11–12).

The final member of the group is Massó, the boarder, who is in love with Nat, but who is scorned by her. He does not appear often, but underlines several important themes.

Bibiana's life alternates between the daily activities associated with her routine and a series of "adventures" which are very out of the ordinary for her. These are cleverly juxtaposed so that the reader can follow Bibiana's train of thoughts as she tries to cope with the new situation by thinking of her home life or tries to ignore it by thinking of domestic problems. The result is both pathetic and amusing. One of these adventures happens the day she goes to the store and is chosen to appear on a radio program and win prizes for having bought Red Cow butter, which, in fact, she had only picked up in order to ask its price. Bibiana cannot believe what is happening and thinks it is all a dream.

Bibiana Prats cannot remember what happened. So much noise . . . Everyone looked at her and she began to get frightened. Her head whirled. She was congratulated, hugged . . . . The women asked her things and looked at how much she had bought. They all told her that they were going to run home because it is always more thrilling to hear a program when you know the woman who is going to speak, when you have seen with your own eyes how everything began. Bibiana, bewildered, did not understand." (p. 81)

Next she is spirited into a car, and characteristically is too confused to ask where she is going. She reacts with mixed fright and pleasure, but her thoughts continually return to her domestic situation, a memory which offers the most security at the moment; she thinks of the buttons she must sew, of the lunch she should be preparing (p. 82). She is genuinely surprised when she learns she is to appear on the radio program. Once she gets onto the stage, though, she suddenly feels her importance and insists on greeting her neighbors and family. "Bibiana Prats is completely happy at this moment. Happy, because she feels she is the heroine of something. An important person. Like any of those American women who lead an active social life" (p. 94).

Bibiana returns to reality when she gets home. The family is very worried, since they do not know what has happened to her, and all descend on her with questions. The woman tries to explain: "The Red Cow! . . . It got me in the market . . . Neither Marcelo nor the boys have a very vivid imagination, but they all think the same thing: A cow escaped from the slaughter house and trampled Bibiana in the Market" (p. 99). After this bit of humor, everyone calms down, and the children complain because dinner is not ready. Thus life returns to normal, except for Bibiana, who views her vulgar, comical adventure in retrospect as her first incursion into "liberated" womanhood: "A woman should . . . well, just this: do what they all do, because men don't ever appreciate that she's stuck at home, always working like a slave, of course . . . ." (p. 105).

Her adventure with the Red Cow reveals an important aspect of her personality: the inability to cope with a strange situation. A later episode is even more indicative of the way she lets herself be dragged along by circumstances. One morning she meets a casual acquaintance who extends an invitation in rather vague terms: "Listen, tomorrow you must come with me . . . It is necessary to get women organized [. . . .] A lot of women are coming . . . very good people, you know. We may even get in to see the Minister" (p. 231). On the strength of this, Bibiana allows herself to be involved in a women's demonstration, without even knowing what she is protesting, or the true implications of her participation. She views it in terms of her only other exciting experience, the radio program, and naively assumes that she will participate in somewhat the same way: "Bibiana Prats is ashamed of not knowing just exactly what she is doing, because she still does not know the object of this stroll, or demonstration or show-of-solidarity or whatever they want to call it. Therefore she abstains from making any comment. Anyway, it seems stupendous to her to take part in a public act, be something in society, she who is so insignificant" (p. 241). But as the women are arrested one by one, Bibiana realizes she may have made a mistake:

> Bibiana Prats doesn't like what is happening at all. The thing is turning out bad. Her initial boldness and camaraderie have disappeared and the only thing she wants to do is to get out of this, return home, finish preparing the meal for her husband and children and hear José's jokes: "Mother, what are these potatoes filled with?" Sometimes José gets boring with the same old song . . . "Well, with meat, of course, what else would potatoes be stuffed with? Not much meat. With the price of meat . . . But, while we're at it, aren't they good?" (p. 241)

This is a typical instance in which a crisis or unfamiliar situation prompts Bibiana to turn her thoughts towards home and the routine in which she is safest. Her ventures into the "social world" generally end like this.

She is jailed and questioned. Her innocence and unfeigned astonishment at learning from the policeman that this was a Communist demonstration convince them of her innocence. She is released, but fined a large sum which Marcelo finally pays.

The novel ends with an episode which is symbolic of Bibiana's life and her relationship with the family. It is the day of the Prats's anniversary. Marcelo starts the day by grabbing Bibiana and wrestling with her on the bed. Bibiana, although flattered, checks his amorous advances, saying that the children are up, but Marcelo continues laughing, saying, "I'll be waiting for you tonight. I'll get you . . . We'll see if you think your husband is a feeble old man. I'm telling you that tonight . . ." (p. 308). His words set the tone for the day and the couple's mood is one of celebration and expectation. Even Marcelo is excited at the thought of their forthcoming festivities; the children are to stay at home, Bibiana receives a gift of material for a dress. She thinks immediately of the children: "I was thinking that this cloth, for Natalia" (p. 319). Marcelo insists that the present is for her alone, perhaps his way of recognizing her sacrifices for the family.

Marcelo buys his wife an elaborate dinner, takes her to a movie, treats her to after-dinner drinks. Bibiana, already tipsy, becomes more and more excited; she wants to walk in the Moncloa gardens, visit an amusement park there, and go dancing. Although he indulges her, Marcelo becomes more and more tired and slows down as the evening wears on. He finally tells her, "Come on, I'll pay and

we'll go home. All I want to do is get to bed. How I want to!" (p. 339).
His wife misinterprets the meaning of the phrase. As they go home
on the subway, Bibiana thinks with anticipation of Marcelo's words
of the morning—thoughts rather unlike her, since on other occasions
she considered marital relations as no more than part of the duties of
a wife. "Bibiana laughs. She wets her lips. She looks at Marcelo
mischievously. She thinks: 'What a man that one is. "Let's see if you
think that your husband is a feeble old man. I'll get you tonight . . ."
that Marcelo'" (p. 339).

As they arrive at their apartment, Bibiana thinks with anticipation
of the lovemaking that will complete this wonderful evening.
However, she must first return to her routine : she goes through the
house, checking to see if everything is in order, and then enters the
bedroom and puts on her best nightgown. Marcelo, she believes, is
playing his usual trick and pretending to sleep, to tease her: "Bibiana
knows that Marcelo is pretending to be asleep. Suddenly, he'll turn
around, grab her with force and say to her: 'Ah, you thought that I
was asleep. Come here, old lady. Today is our anniversary. We must
celebrate it.'" She gets into bed, shakes her husband playfully,
then comes to the realization that he is really asleep: "Bibiana
Prats's hands tremble slightly. (No, if I . . . Well, that didn't matter
very much to me truthfully, but I . . .) Marcelo is sweating. His
forehead is wet. Bibiana wipes Marcelo's forehead with the fold of
the sheet.—Marcelo . . . oh, Marcelo" (pp. 344–45).

II   *The Character*

Bibiana is the focal point of the novel. Around her the author
groups the rest of the characters, whose function is to illuminate
different facets of her life at home or in society. Through this character, Miss Medio will comment on Spain's social structure, education,
and human relationships, but Bibiana also lives in her own right.

Bibiana Prats's importance resides in the fact that she is a housewife and aspires to be nothing more. She is unconcerned with events
that do not bear directly on her family circle or her immediate needs.
Her reactions to situations beyond the family scope reveal a limited
mentality, emphasized by the many proverbs and clichés which form
the bulk of her vocabulary, showing little of thought. The reader
must judge these experiences in the light of Bibiana's abilities,
determined in great part by her traditional upbringing.

Perhaps the major trait in Bibiana's character is her lack of a strong personality. She allows herself to be led by circumstances instead of dominating them. To act decisively seems to be alien to her nature, since the role which she has assumed long since involves self-effacement before the family group, and extends into other phases of her life. Thus, her desire to be able to invite her daughter's confidence gives way before her fear of annoying her. For this reason too, she will not invite friends into the house, because "Nat doesn't like Bibiana to bring strange people into the home, not even the neighbors" (p. 134). Even when she is completely responsible for the decision, she cannot act quickly; an example is her agony over how much to tip the old woman selling subway tickets:

> "How much do I have to give you?" The woman says: "Whatever you want." Bibiana Prats doesn't know how much "whatever you want" is . . . Twenty *centavos*? Fifty? Marcelo always says that tips should be ten percent of the bill. Natalia says that ten percent is indicative of stingy people who count everything, who measure everything, who don't want to look bad to people, but who don't have the generosity to furnish happiness with their munificence. Either you give something or don't give anything. José says that tipping is an antisocial act, that it is immoral, like charity. Man has all his rights, and, among them, the right to work and to be justly paid for his work, without being humiliated by alms, that the tip humiliates the one who gives it and the one who receives it. But the fact is that people are very low on money and humiliation doesn't matter very much to them. Xenius gives what he has without thinking. He is like Natalia, although perhaps he doesn't act like that for the same reasons. (p. 182)

Bibiana's life is hermetic because the outside world touches her only when introduced by the family, an arrangement which is totally satisfactory to her. She cannot conceive of activity that is not directly related to her household, with the resultant feelings of insecurity whenever she finds herself in a situation that is alien to her previous experience. The first chapters of the novel present Bibiana's nervous preparations for a party which the children are giving for their friends. The party is a point of convergence between the potentially hostile outside world and the family circle. Bibiana's reactions to the characters provide an intermediate step for her later adventures.

Each time Bibiana ventures out on her own, her experience reveals her complete ignorance of contemporary life and its changing customs. Her upbringing, which obviously had sheltered her from life, and her marriage, a continuation of the same, have fitted her for the home while deliberately creating a gap between home and society. The results of this outlook are verified in many episodes : her first visit alone to the movies, the radio program, and the demonstration aptly prove Bibiana's lack of integration in society.

An inability to see beyond her limited sphere of interest prevents Bibiana from grasping the seriousness of her position. The outside world is "society" to her, and she derives her concept of a modern woman (which she deems herself after appearing on the radio program) from simplistic generalities about social life. The comic element, based on Bibiana's extreme naïvete, is a subtle way of disguising the inherent tragedy : a woman, educated in the traditional mold, whose only interests are her family, is unprepared to understand and participate in contemporary society. The alternation between home life (the predictable routine which provides security) and the drastic results of her introduction to the outside world shows the extent to which she is out of step with the modern world.

Bibiana's sole interest is Marcelo and the children, and so the family brings out the third major trait of her personality: her complete submissiveness to the needs or desires of the family. She sacrifices for the children, protecting them from Marcelo's real or imagined temper. Her idea of a good marriage equates duty and sacrifice with love, and actually gives a resumé of her activities in the novel:

Bibiana Prats would like to be able to explain to her daughter what love is, what she understands by love. She would like to tell her: Don't joke, Nat. Which of the two of us is married, which knows what it is to love a man really, to suffer for him and care for him, to suffer him in bed when you don't feel like it at all, and pretend that you're enjoying it so as not to hurt his feelings? What do you know what it is to want a kiss and never get it, or desire . . . —you know—very much when some days . . . well, just that, and see your man go to sleep in your arms because he is tired or because he has just been with another woman. What do you know! And you are left. . . . ? And you keep quiet and put up with his whims, now I want to and now I don't. And you always smile. What do you know what it is to wait anxiously for a date, a day, which he forgets, or a hug or a word which you expect as a reward for something that the man hasn't even noticed? How could you know what it is to bear his children, care for them when they are sick so he will not worry? And scrub, and wash, and sew the clothes, straining your eyes, so he can waste five *duros* with his friends . . . And prevent unpleasantness between him and his children . . . (p. 219)

This passage explains the reason for Bibiana's actions and sets, in succinct form, the pattern to which she conforms her behavior. The idea of duty and uncomplaining resignation is very strong with her. Her thoughts give her a depth that she has not had up to now, for these words, reinforced by her pathetic resignation at the close of the work, reveal her philosophy of life.

The anniversary scene prompted one critic's harsh condemnation of the novel as scabrous.[2] Yet Dolores Medio's intention was obviously not to create the atmosphere of an erotic novel. This is one of the few times in which Bibiana has allowed herself to think only of her legitimate pleasure. She has entered wholly into the situation, letting herself be carried away by the moment. But at the time when she lets herself go completely, at the very moment when the author could have ended the novel on a sentimental note, she chose to cut the consummation short with a very undramatic, prosaic incident: Marcelo's tiredness causes him to fall asleep. This is the very point of the novel: by rejecting the unusual and concentrating on what would be a rather expectable situation (an older man tired after a great deal of excitement), she most accurately portrays her idea of everyday life in all its realism. The reader thus receives the detailed portrait of Bibiana's uneventful life. With characteristic resignation, she does not insult her husband or cry out at the irony of the situation. Her disappointment is obvious from the buildup of her expectations and from her final words, yet the way she accepts the situation provides a note of true pathos.

The choice of the anniversary to demonstrate this point is masterly. By using a celebration which traditionally signifies renewal, the author has suggested that Bibiana will continue unprotestingly to accept her frustrated existence and the sacrifice it entails. Resignation and submissiveness mark Bibiana's characteristic attitudes within the family group, no matter how unsatisfactory the relationships may be.

III   *Human Interaction in* Bibiana

The Prats family is a microcosm through which Miss Medio studies the nature of human relationships. Bibiana serves as the buffer between the head of the household and the rest of the family. There appears to be no real understanding among the members of the family, and Bibiana must mediate in order to keep the family running smoothly. Marcelo, especially, makes no effort to understand the spiritual needs of his children; he feels he has done more than his share in providing for them physically. The thought of treating the children as beings in their own right is not part of his idea of a parental relationship. He thus refuses to understand the sensitive Xenius, and alludes to his "homosexual" propensity for poetry, which is both unmanly and unprofitable:

> "What this idiot may become in life . . . A Poet. Just what we needed . . . A poet! Starving to death . . . Tell me whenever has poetry been profitable . . . Look, I would rather . . ."
> Anger chokes Marcelo, making him stutter. . . .
> ". . . have him turn out to be a Communist, that's it, a Communist, rather than a poet . . ." (p. 197)

Thus a study of family interaction leads into one of the main themes of the work: the lack of communication, already strongly developed in the parallel work, *Public Servant*. It is impossible for the family to reach one another except on the most elementary level. Although continual sympathy would seem abnormal—no family lives in complete harmony—there is a very pathetic undercurrent in the need for companionship which is underscored by later analogues concerning characters only remotely connected with the family. A gesture of understanding would make the difference, but that gesture is not forthcoming. Marcelo's obvious disappointment in Xenius contributes much to the family strife, but Bibiana's loneliness provides an even better case, for although she is needed to provide for the family wants, she does not communicate with them well. She is afraid to approach Nat, for fear of the girl's cold rebuffs. Marcelo's conversations seem limited to complaints and the desire for food; their anniversary celebration ends in disappointment for Bibiana. Marcelo also adds to the general atmosphere of alienation, for he refuses to accept any reasons which do not conform with his own interests (Xenius' poetical inclinations, Natalia's desires to rise in the world). Miss Medio comments on his lack of perception, hinting at a depth in Xenius that Marcelo is not capable of understanding: "[. . .] what does he know of Xenius, of his sadness, his bitterness, his strange and special kind of existence?" (p. 15).

Massó provides the most pathetic note of the family group. He is the objective correlative to this theme: physically part of the family because he rents a room, but spiritually alone. He is in love with Nat, and even proposes to her (a move suspected and approved by the parents) but is brusquely rejected by her over and over again. His loneliness is not allayed by being with the Prats and he seemingly can gain attention only with his presents, as when he wins acceptance at the party given by the children when he buys refreshments. He is actually trying to impress Nat, but the gesture has the opposite effect: "Natalia doesn't smile. She doesn't say anything. She thinks: ('The old fool . . . What is he doing here? He's always meddling in what isn't his business . . . Mama is to blame for all this, for allowing him to get into everything, for not having put him out in the street by now.')" (p. 51). However, the others draw him into the party, talk to him, dance with him: "Lorenzo Massó feels like someone important. For a thousand *pesetas* he has bought the friendship of the boys and girls. Now he has the upper hand" (p. 56).

A casual acquaintance affords still another view of man's loneliness. Bibiana ventures to the movies alone for the first time, and meets Eladia, a young woman who lives in a rented room and has no friends. She strikes up a conversation with Bibiana and will not let her go, inviting her for a drink to postpone the hour when she will be alone again. Although aware of this, Bibiana does not invite her into the Prats's apartment, even when the girl hints for an invitation:

> They stop in front of the house. Bibiana hesitates. She doesn't want to invite her to come up to see her. Nat doesn't like Bibiana to bring unknown people into the home, not even the neighbors . . . Eladia Suárez is in no hurry to leave Bibiana Prats. She is a very agreeable woman and Eladia Suárez is very alone. But the agreeable woman has to cook dinner and tries, once again, to say goodbye. . . . They say goodbye. Bibiana sees her go off walking slowly as if with no direction, with her hands in her pockets, her purse hanging from her arm, her kerchief a little twisted . . . (Alone . . . What a life! I wasn't very nice. Well, people also have their obligations . . . Good Heavens! Dinner . . .). (pp. 134–35)

This is still another example of how each person is wrapped up in his own interests, and is either unaware of the other's need or is unwilling to make the effort to help the other.

IV   *The Individual and Society*

The patterns established within the Prats family are reflections of Spanish society. A radical indifference to the needs of others, the refusal to work for improvement because of inertia or fear of resultant insecurity operates on an individual and collective level. The family educates the children to conform to behavior which promotes self-interest.

Society has its victims, natural products of the rigid economical system. The impassivity with which it treats these people implies the continuation of such patterns, which preclude rebellion and only require unhesitating submission for their persistence. The family imitates the same type of behavior on the individual level. Bibiana is the victim of a structure which she willingly supports, accepting her position as one of duty.

The problems inherent to the class to which the Prats family belongs and the representative mentality of the lower middle class justify classifying *Bibiana* as a social novel. Prats, who had inherited a small shop, feels very strongly about providing a practical education for his children : they must be able to make a living in the world. Marcelo is also keenly aware of his situation compared with others'. He believes that the government provides a much easier life for the employee: "Some life the government employees have! Leaves, vacations, insurance, group benefits and all that . . ." (p. 165). He also speaks of the dilemma of the small shopkeeper who must compete with large stores and mass production: "You think things are like they were in your aunt's lifetime . . . Those were other times . . . It was a business. Now the large department stores monopolize everything . . . Everything is cheaper. They buy in bulk and they even manufacture. Who can compete with them? To heck with the small businessman" (p. 164).

He thus feels that the best education he can give his children is to show them how to fight for their rights; for this reason he insists that little Manuel stand up to the neighborhood bully even though he is frightened :

> It hurts Marcelo to have his children made fun of because he knows, by experience, what is what. He never confessed it, but Bibiana knows that more than once he has been cheated and abused in word and deed for not having dared to answer with force. He lost what was his by cowardice. Bibiana knows it. That's why Marcelo Prats wants his children to know how to defend themselves. Life is the best teacher. Perhaps the most immoral, but the best. (p. 287)

For once, Bibiana sides with her husband in the matter: "Bibiana doesn't say anything, She loves Manuel as much as his father.

More than his father. She carried him in her belly. She gave birth to him with pain . . . But she recognizes that his father is right. The boy is to live in society. Among other boys. Among other men. And the world belongs to the strongest." (pp. 289–90) These words, so alien to Bibiana's usual soft character, underline the preoccupation which besets both parents.

Yet even within the instinct for self-protection there is another hidden, subconscious motive which also adds to the commentary on Spanish social structure in *Bibiana*:

> In the defensive attitude that Marcelo Prats recommends to his son, there is an ancestral hatred of centuries, a thirst for revenge, for rebellion, which sleeps crouched in the deepest part of Marcelo Prats's subconscious, which his conscious reasoning could not stifle . . . Many generations of oppression, of humiliations, of servitude, cry out in the voice of the man when he advises his child to rebel against the rich boy who taunts him.
>
> There is the case: the rich boy. The issue would not have had such importance if it were a question of another boy of his class. (288–89)

Thus the first hint of a certain social dissatisfaction—resentment of a lower class for the upper—appears in *Bibiana*. Although it has not been accorded much space, one cannot help but feel that it is a central issue: It is the reason why the children must attend school, the reason Natalia is so anxious to rise above her station, the reason why Marcelo works so hard. This feeling is passed on, for when the fight ends in a draw, and the rich boy extends his hand in friendship, Manuel spits on the ground and turns his back (pp. 295–96). His refusal to be reconciled, to attempt to understand, appears more worthy to his peers than the ethically superior gesture of the rich boy, and Manuel is now accepted as one of the group.

V *Continuing Philosophy, Changing Focus*

Although critical reactions to *Bibiana* have been quite favorable, few have discussed the implicit criticism of the social system that it has represented. Most reviews concentrate on external elements of technique, which show advances over the previous works. The creation of the environment which surrounds and is responsible for producing a character like Bibiana is a product of painstaking investigation and a great knack for details. Touches like the conversations out the window with the neighbors, the chronicle of Bibiana's daily chores, the routine of the family, and especially the quick sketches of other minor characters give a richness to the background which raises it to a level of prime importance. It also suggests that the novel was intended to be a panoramic description of a social class, with Bibiana as the cohesive element, rather than a study of a woman of the middle class.

As in previous works, the author offers a wide range of quick, vivid sketches which have an artistic and documentary value per se. There are many representatives of the lower middle class in *Bibiana* and their attitudes are diverse but typical: Nat's desperate attempts to rise above her class; Eladia's pathetic situation as a lonely girl in Madrid; the recurring theme of the sublessee with Eladia and Massó; the role of each family member and his responsibility to himself and the others. There are quick glimpses into the scenes of everyday life: chatting across the inner courtyard from the windows, going to the movies, preparing dinner for the family. The abundance of such detailed scenes prompted one critic to classify *Bibiana* as a *novela de costumbres*[3] rather than as a social novel where most other critics have placed it.[4] It is difficult to separate the two types neatly, since the realistic presentation of a specific class and its problems would naturally include the description of its customs and activities. Yet the primary intention of *Bibiana* is not strictly description for its own sake. The sketches take second place to the composite picture of class attitude.

Each of these scenes provides a different focus on life in the middle class, and more specifically, reflects possibilities which Bibiana discards as wrong. Nat, the modern woman, "liberated" in her own way, refuses to conform to the traditional mold; Xenius rebels against his father's pragmatic attitudes with his poetry; the oldest son has strong Socialist or Communist leanings. These children will not conform to values to which their parents cling, and through them Miss Medio develops her philosophy concerning the instability of the middle class. Other signs of rebellion are the women's demonstration and the changing mores and values of the younger generation.

In her chronicle of the middle class, Miss Medio has naturally turned to elements which she has successfully employed before, and therefore there are some parallels with *Public Servant*, the other novel of this type. The urban setting is common to both, as the milieu par excellence for this class; the daily routine emphasizes her interest in describing insignificant people as well as actions which, multiplied many times, comprise the majority of the population; both Bibiana and Pablo Marín are average and representative rather than atypical; both are indecisive as well, have no great ambition, and are confined to a narrow circle of reality by their own volition. Common themes— both social and human—unite the two (the concern for money, the sublessee, the themes of noncommunication and misunderstanding). Similar techniques also link *Public Servant* and *Bibiana*: a realistic description, the emphasis on the commonplace, a chronicle of daily activities.

The differences, however, are more telling than the similarities. The structure of *Public Servant* centers on a series of ups and downs based on Pablo's dreams and reality. The work ends in a self-revelation and his affirmative acknowledgment of his position in society after a momentary rebellion. *Bibiana*, on the other hand, never deviates from its understated emotional level, with hardly a variation from the monotony of existence. Even Bibiana's adventures (actually parodies of any real "adventure") must end in the boredom of routine.

Although the endings of the two works differ in focus (the first with a climax, the other, with anticlimax), the general philosophy remains constant. Although the work naturally lends itself to analysis in terms of its social or representational import, its descriptive elements, or even the importance of the epoch in which it is situated, one can see above all Miss Medio's continuing interest in the person as a whole. For this, we can return to the author's own insistence on the importance of man above and beyond the theoretical and trace it to Ortega y Gasset's "vital philosophy." This novel corroborates the author's concern with the human side of the questions, for no matter what class problem she presents, she always chooses an individual to represent it and make it more immediate. The words that preface the novel thus become clearer. She again turns to Ortega for inspiration with the phrase "A perfect mother would be an ideal of a mother. But to be a mother is not to be ideal." Thus Bibiana is seen in the multiple roles which comprise her life—mother, wife, friend, individual—but the varying perspectives of each role must take second place to the more human side, subject to foibles, errors and mistakes, as well as the loyalty and noble sense of duty which guide her. And it is always with this in mind that Dolores Medio creates her characters. With such a presentation, she strives to win the reader's sympathy for these vulgar, insignificant heroes, and to teach him to become more sensitive to the difficulties of living and to the needs of his fellow creatures.

CHAPTER 9

Short Narrative 1966–1971

I El señor García

ALTHOUGH *The Fish Stays Afloat* may be considered an artistic orchestration of many short self-contained episodes, Miss Medio did not return to the true short narrative until the publication of the novelette *El señor García (Mr. García)* in 1966.[1] It has certain affinities with *Public Servant*: both have male protagonists, both hold white collar jobs in Madrid, have economic problems, and hope for more money in their work. The similarity touches the manner of presentation too : the approach to the subject is from the point of view of the protagonist.

The plot line is minimal: José García has worked his way up in the Company from errand boy to general office worker. The head of his office is soon to be promoted, and informs García that he is to take over his job, which means a considerable amount of prestige and a salary more than double his present one. García is over-whelmed and, although he intends to keep the news a secret until it is official, he soon blurts it out. He spends his lunch hour planning his new life : he makes out a new budget, thinks of changing his dreary lodging; having the means to date women, and of finally reaping the reward for his efforts.

This is a clear case of counting chickens before they are hatched, but José is not alone in anticipating the benefits of his good fortune. His co-workers suddenly become more friendly, and the girl whom he has admired from afar shows an interest in him at last. After work, he returns to his home of many years, an apartment where he sublets and shares an airless room with two other men. He tells his landlady about the raise but she anticipates his desire to leave and insists on giving him the dining room which she intends to renovate into a bed-room for him, maternally solicitous about his well-being. During his first night in the makeshift bedroom, he is startled to find the land-lady's daughter sitting next to him; she shamelessly forces herself on him. The next day García learns that the job has been given to a man who has connections with the board of directors.

The action of the story takes place in approximately twenty-four hours, but the short space of time and limited number of pages contain great density of emotional content. Most of the work explores García's reaction to the good news. The use of temporal contrasts heightens the protagonist's excited reaction. García considers the present as a limbo from which he soon will be released, and his thoughts shift between past (memory) and future (possibility). For example, Miss Medio devotes one section to a detailed description of García's lunch hour: the crowded restaurant, the table shared with strangers, the same inexpensive meal. Now, however, he gives himself over to thoughts of his new position: he stops at a cafe, orders brandy, and decides that from now on he will have meat and dessert at his noonday meal.

García, like Pablo Marín of *Public Servant* or the protagonists of the other short stories, cannot help but be dominated by circumstances; like the others, he is one of the "ordinary" people who do not assert themselves and for this reason are swept along by the current of life, not daring to protest. The lunch table scene provides an ironic example of this: in celebration, García decides to vary his monotonous fare, but the waiter, familiar with García's routine, doesn't give him a chance to state his preference, and calls in the usual order. "José García is going to say something, but he doesn't dare. He ends up by resigning himself to eating stew . . . ('This is a special day . . . I'll order dessert')" (pp. 38–39). The protagonist does not get satisfaction in this case either. Accustomed to having his client leave without dessert, the waiter gives him the bill, and again García does not dare protest: "José García is left without dessert. He doesn't dare tell Pedro that things have changed for him and that he intends to add dessert to his meals [. . .]" (p. 41). Almost the same pattern occurs at the apartment : he intends to leave, but the landlady takes control of the situation and manipulates events so that he will stay; her daughter also dominates him despite his rather feeble protests. Thus the present is determined in great measure by past events; it is not so easy for the man to break away from the routine. He must be strong enough to face—and even defy—circumstances, but he is not able.

García's meagre salary, his inferior position and dull existence make his anticipation even more poignant. His excitement is contagious, and the reader cannot help but be caught up in this drama, for the identification with the character by means of a spontaneous sympathy : the author presents the facts, but does not direct the reader's opinion. Miss Medio has succeeded in eliminating her presence from the work so that the reader has direct contact with the protagonist, a technique necessary for the maximum emotional impact on the reader when García learns the bad news. Given a limited range of omniscience (the third-person exposition hardly includes any direct commentary or author intrusion), the reader receives the same impression of surprise as García.

The ironic ending is typical of the earlier short stories and especially "Tomorrow," in which, it will be remembered, another protagonist of the same class learns that she is not the master of her own fate. García's reaction to the news adds pathos to the story. He used to laugh at the director's witticisms even though they were not funny. One that particularly rankled him was a joke concerning his name: they called him a "foreigner" (because José García is such a typically Spanish name), but he would always laugh because it pleased and flattered the teller. After informing García that another is taking over the job, the director airs his joke for the newcomer, referring to García in the same way:

> The foreigner, as your father-in-law says . . . You have a foreigner working in your office . . . Ha, Ha, I'm saying it because of your name.
> José García says: "Very clever."
> He would like to laugh louder because Mr. Fontecha is very nice. But the laughter doesn't come out of his throat. He says only: "Ha" (p. 130)

The novelette ends with those words, creating a circular narrative, since *Mr. García* begins when the protagonist tries to anticipate Fontecha's jokes and flatter him with his laughter. Fontecha brings up the same joke after telling him the news about his promotion: "You know what I'm thinking? That someone will ask us if the new boss of these offices is a foreigner" (p. 17). This time, however, García has reason to be appreciative.

Other patterns, constant subthemes in Miss Medio's literature, appear in *Mr. García*: group dynamics seen in intraoffice relationships, the problems of the subtenant, the lack of family warmth and needed privacy; constant economic pressures and worries, solitude and absence of communication, indifference toward others and self-interest which precludes sympathy or understanding.

García is one of the anonymous mass that Miss Medio has devoted herself to describing. He is colorless and ordinary in the same way as Pablo—even his name is purposely undistinguished. He is to be confused with many others like him who have suffered the same abuses and treatment; they have also been ignored and unloved. Perhaps the concision of this work makes the protagonist even more sympathetic than Pablo Marín. By concentrating on a single aspect of García's life, Miss Medio focuses on the pathetic and unjust elements which affect the little man, who cannot even protest his treatment.

II *Andrés*

One year later, Miss Medio published an outstanding collection of short stories under the titles of *Andrés*, for which she received one of the more prestigious prizes awarded for short stories, the Premio Sésamo.[2]

Andrés is the young son of a paralytic father who is unable to work. Tormented by the suspicion that his mother is keeping the family by prostitution, Andrés follows her one day. When he realizes that it is true, with a precocious sense of honor he insists that she return home. At first she protests her innocence, but tiring at last, she admits the truth. Andrés finally convinces his mother to let him support the family, even though he must sacrifice his schooling.

The mother considers prostitution coldly, as a necessity. Her attitude exposes what economic need can do to a person's outlook and morals. The lack of emotion on her part contrasts with Andrés' rapid maturing, his emotional approach to the question of honor, and his desire to take his place as the breadwinner. Miss Medio emphasizes the sordidness with which Andrés associates prostitution in the description of the apartment in which they live : the faded tablecloth with the hole in it, the grease spot on the cloth, the glass with fingerprints on it, are details which suggest that cleanliness and perfection have changed to lack of caring and apathy.

In "Andrés" and other stories in this collection, Miss Medio has captured the speech forms of the lower class with great skill, giving an air of almost documentary realism by exposition through dialogue.

A young boy is also the protagonist of "La segunda vez" ("The Second Time"). Nine-year-old Joaquín is beset with money problems : he must sell the cookies his mother makes. Outside a cafe, another boy accidentally upsets Joaquín's tray and the merchandise is crushed and ruined, but the boy's tears arouse the sympathy of the clientele, who make up a collection of ninety *pesetas*—even more than the child expected for the entire day's work. Thrilled with the happy ending of his potential tragedy, Joaquín decides to create the same circumstances again, and deliberately bumps into a foreigner in another cafe. Unfortunately, just as this group is getting out their wallets, a client from the first cafe exposes the fraud and the boy runs away.

The obsession with money is the prime moving force in the story. Joaquín is not interested in becoming rich, but simply living on the survival level, and is willing to resort to trickery. The writer makes no moral judgments here, but solely presents the adventure from the point of view of the child, ending with this thought, "What a scare! And it all seemed so simple . . ." (p. 36).

"Injusticia" ("Injustice") also deals with poverty, but presents the other side of the moral picture in a magnificent exposition of the struggle between desire and duty. Thirteen-year-old Pablo works long hours selling candy in a movie house; he earns very little money for his effort, but at times is the sole support of his family. This evening he stumbles on a wallet stuffed with money, which turns his existence from then on into a tormented question : should he keep the money or return it? After a week of vacillation, he decides to turn it in to the police station, but instead of praise for his honesty, he receives suspicious treatment and harsh words because he didn't report the find immediately. Comments the author: "How can Pablo explain to the police commissioner his vacillation, his doubts, his latent desire, which he himself is not aware of, all the trouble it was for him to overcome this desire. How can the commissioner suspect that before him stands a little hero, a child who has won all by himself one of the most difficult battles in life, if the child himself doesn't even realize it?" (p. 56)

Miss Medio thus emphasizes the moral struggle of a child whose upbringing had condoned wrongdoing: "His father says that everyone steals something in life and keeping what one finds is something that isn't very important" (p. 52). Miss Medio presents Pablo's fantasies about what he could do with the money : he would realize his dream of owning a taxi, buy furniture, provide a house and clothing for his family. Most of all, he would buy food, since they never have enough to eat, and the children go to bed hungry. Miss Medio points out the irony of the situation: "Pablo and Pedro go to sleep again. Under the pillows of the two boys who have fallen asleep without satisfying their hunger there is a wallet that contains five bills of one thousand *pesetas*, four of one hundred and some small ones. Five thousand, four hundred sixty-seven *pesetas* and thirty *céntimos* to be exact" (p. 53). Each one of these *pesetas* could assuage the children's hunger, satisfy the needs of the entire family, and for that reason the author emphasizes the quantity which in turn suggests the implicit comparison. The stress on the different denominations suggests that Pablo has counted these bills many times, with only his moral doubts between the money and his hunger.

Miss Medio also provides further contrast on the ethical level. The decision to return the wallet finally brings Pablo peace of mind:

He walks lightly. Almost content. Yes, content. He is content. He is happy. There won't be a lot of food. There won't be a car . . . or whatever. He will be poor as a churchmouse again, he will take a few pennies for his expenses from his tips before handing them over to his mother. But he is content. His uneasiness has disappeared. He has won a battle which lets him feel that he is a man and a responsible one." (p. 55)

The only reward for his honesty—self-satisfaction—soon disappears after his experience at the police station. His disillusionment is a lesson taught by life, which no doubt will happen again: "Pablo returns to the street a bit bewildered. The injustice hurts him. An injustice of which no one is guilty. That's life. Perhaps if he had kept the money he wouldn't have had to justify anything. But then . . . " (p. 57).

"La fuina" ("The Marten") describes another traumatic experience which marks the inevitable initiation into manhood. Young Lalo has received a shotgun as a present, and now he must prove he is a man by killing the marten which has been decimating the family's chickens. As he waits in the dark for the animal to come, he remembers some revolting episodes he witnessed recently: his visit to a farm where a bull and cow were mated; his intuition that sex was not confined only to animals; a servant girl whom his mother recently discharged and who now was obviously pregnant. Intuitively, he knows that his mother also must have a knowledge of sex, since he and his brothers are proof of this. He is shaken from these thoughts by a noise in the night, but to his surprise he realizes that these are not animal sounds. He hears sighs, panting, and finally two forms separate from the shadows. Lalo fires at one of them. Although later he says he thought it was the marten, it is obvious that the act of shooting is his symbolic rebellion against growing up, symbolized by the sexual act.

"¿Vamos, Timoteo?" ("Shall We Go, Timoteo?") describes the unhappy experience of a boy from a poor family who, like Andrés of the first story, is anxious to retire his mother from a life of prostitution. He saves to invest in four plastic toys, circus cyclists which he baptizes with the name of Timoteo, and he demonstrates their skill outdoors on a wire tied around a tree. He draws a crowd, and just as they show some interest in buying, a car drives onto the sidewalk and crushes his merchandise, thus smashing his hopes of saving his mother. The chauffeur refuses to pay for the damage.

The story is extremely pathetic, contrasting the boy's expectations and the final result, and providing a glimpse into the way others take advantage of poverty (the crowd can see he is in rags and is suffering from chilblains, but insists on bargaining for the toys at a ridiculously low price). Finally, the author connects the boy with so many others in his class by a kind of determinism that inexorably makes them losers in life: someone is always waiting to take advantage of them, or at the very least, refuses to recognize the need of those who suffer. This concept is translated into the boy's idea of life as a circus. He recalls his father's words: "that life was like a circus, where some laugh and have a good time, because they pay, and others make them laugh with their clownishness, where some hit hard because they can do it and others always receive the blows. Yes, that is what his father said. Juan thinks that life is like a circus and he is a clown" (p. 80). This hierarchy, so clear in the child's mind, is apparent in most of Miss Medio's work treating the lower classes.

"Cuesta arriba" ("Uphill") is another tale about an unhappy child whose misunderstanding of a situation causes a tragedy. Young Tomás is accustomed to carrying his paralyzed sister on his back wherever he goes, but learns to his dismay that she is to be sent to a clinic. Actually, the doctor has suggested a place where she can be rehabilitated, but the boy doesn't understand this, and can only think of insane asylums with mistreated inmates. He therefore carries her off up the hill to a nearby woods. At night a search party comes to look for them, and Tomás, running away, falls from a cliff with the girl on his back.

"¡Hola, jefe!" ("Hi, Boss!") reveals the child's inability to gauge the magnitude of his actions, which, in this case, infringe upon an adult world where the rules are necessarily different. Young Claudio waits on tables in a bar, and longs for the day when he will tend bar and be the cashier like Eloy. What most infuriates him is that Eloy seems to keep some of the tip money for himself. In order to get rid of Eloy, Claudio accuses him of stealing from the till. He is fired, and Claudio only realizes the enormity of his deed when he learns of the stigma that follows a person who has been dismissed without references. After a struggle with his own conscience (after all, Eloy did steal), Claudio admits to his lie. The story ends "happily," with Claudio assured that he too can keep some of the tip money when he assumes Eloy's position one day. Claudio contentedly envisions his future as the "boss."

"El organillo" ("The Hand Organ") is what Rafael's mother plays in front of the cafes. She is pregnant, abandoned by her husband, and must support several children. Rafael helps her by collecting the money, while she goes through the farce of saying dispirited *olé's* to accompany the music. Today, she feels labor pains while they are in downtown Madrid, and despite the efforts to get her home, she has the baby in the entrance hall of a building. She and the infant are taken to a Maternity Hospital and Rafael begins his rounds with the organ and burro. His growth and initiation into manhood came about by seeing the mystery of birth and he is now the official breadwinner.

"El más fuerte" ("The Strongest One") is based on an episode described in *Bibiana*, in which the father, Marcelo, forced little Manolo to fight with the neighborhood bully. This story, however, lacks the strong social implications of the novelistic episode, and concentrates on the victory as a symbol of manhood. The rural setting provides a different background, but otherwise the elements are almost identical: Young Matías' father insists that he fight with the boy who has been bullying him, or else he will always be considered a coward. Much against his will, he does so and wins, thus gaining the admiration of the other boys. His initiation into manhood is acknowledged by his father as he invites the boy to join the adult workers and use the dangerous scythe.

"Un capote para Braulio" ("A Cape for Braulio") again treats the incongruous distance between dreams and reality. Braulio is an apprentice to a construction gang, but he yearns to be a bullfighter. This desire, however, has nothing to do with money, but with the symbolism of the sport. He distinguishes himself one day by leaping into the bullring and getting arrested for his efforts, but he is satisfied that he has shown the world that he is not a coward in what counts the most, even though he does get vertigo when he is high in the construction. He is welcomed as a conquering hero on his return to the job, and his co-workers jokingly promise that they will form a special cheering section for him when he becomes famous, and if he is killed in the ring, they will buy him a cape to cover his body. That very day, Braulio dies in a fall. The men remember their words, but since the boy has not died in the ring, it seems foolish to buy a cape. One of the men gently covers the body with an empty cement sack, and places his work helmet on Braulio's chest, a silent tribute to his death in the line of duty and an ironic parallel to his dreams of glory.

"La última zambomba" ("The Last Toy Drum") returns to the theme of initiation into manhood, in this case through the camaraderie of his fellow workers, whom José joins for a noisy Christmas Eve celebration. He takes his *zambomba* (a crudely made drum) with him, and after some rowdy merrymaking in the streets, the men go to a girl's house for dancing and drinking. José gets so drunk that he passes out and doesn't remember what happened, although he feels he is now as much of a man as any of them. When he returns home, suffering from a hangover, his little brother is waiting for him and asks for the *zambomba*, which José says he broke from so much playing (actually he left it at the woman's house, but is ashamed to return and ask for it). "Besides, it wasn't worth anything . . . Bah! Just a toy drum," (p. 256) thus definitely separating his world from that of childhood.

The last story, "El botones" ("The Bellboy"), contrasts feelings of self-respect and happiness which soon turn into disillusionment. Young Felipe has been initiated into the mysteries of sex by an American woman who kept him as a gigolo for a while, then suddenly dropped him in favor of another. Although he is sorry to lose the material luxuries that accompanied the affair, his pride is hurt because of the slight to his dignity. His experience may have made him a man, but despite his efforts to remain impassive, he wipes two large tears from his eyes.

The child or adolescent boy provides the obvious unity in this collection, but the emotional atmosphere also forms a second theme: these stories expose the sad or pathetic side of human nature or of life. Many characters have grown up too fast, their childhood prematurely truncated by the burden of work at an early age; some are

lost in a world of adult values; some are made to realize the dispro-
portionate distance between dreams and reality; for some the transition process to manhood is extremely painful (through violence or
sex); finally having attained manhood, some are disillusioned by
what the adult world represents. Contrast provides the reader with
two different worlds which are contiguous but which apparently
cannot coincide: the potential world of childhood (one of dreams,
of play, of happiness) and the real world (one of necessity, hunger,
need, and violence).

The author's ability to economize on details and concentrate on
the emotional tone of the story is noteworthy in this collection.
What interests her is not the question in the abstract, but the actual
effect of the problem on the protagonist, and it is all the more
poignant since many times the child himself is unaware of the implications of his action. He acts almost instinctively, and it is up to
the reader to see the enormous injustices perpetrated upon the
children who are allowed to mature all too quickly, who become men
before they even become adolescents.

Miss Medio also emphasizes the human interest by setting up contrasts between the situation as described "objectively" and the protagonist's subjective view of it. Interior monologues and thought
patterns interspersed with third-person exposition provide the shifting perspective between the subject and his experience. To eliminate
her presence as much as possible, the author also concentrates on
transcribing speech that fits the status of her characters. Popular
slang, coarse expressions, numerous proverbs, half-finished thoughts
and sentences provide a convincing rendition of the speech of a child
of the lower classes.

III   Uncollected Short Stories

Having discovered a successful means of creating the illusion of
reality through lower-class speech and thought patterns, Miss Medio
erases author presence entirely in a completely monologic short story
entitled "Tira, Nicolasa" ("Giddy-up, Nicolasa").[3] An elderly man
recollects the old days when mechanization had not reigned supreme,
and a man's worth was measured in human rather than mechanical
terms. These reminiscences are confided to Nicolasa, his burro, as
they walk down the road homeward. Ironically, time and again they
are forced off the road by fast-moving vehicles, symbolic of their

inferior position in the scale of life's values. The old man consoles himself with the thought that with or without a machine, we all must die.

Miss Medio provides a literal transcription of the old man's ramblings, complete with thoughts on politics, the war, the changing times, numerous proverbs, colorful insults at the passing motorists, a thumbnail sketch of his own life, rhetorical questions, and snatches of a song. The technique of having a simple country person pose the important economic and social question (the effect of progress on Spain and specifically the rapid changes in the country) poignantly reveals how large-scale change can effect the small person, who is not interested in or aware of more wide-reaching implications.

"El puñado de yerba seca" ("The Handful of Dry Grass"), from the same year, also chronicles a social change from the point of view of the individual affected by it.[4] The move from the country to the city, with its attraction of good wages and a more comfortable life, is an economic reality in Spain today. Martín and his family are living examples : his wife had insisted on the change, reinforcing her point with stories of a good life, comfortable housing, and an education for the children. Martín reluctantly gives in, sells everything, and takes a job with a large company in Avilés. However, he is not truly satisfied with his decision, for he still feels the pull of the land, and as they arrive near the outskirts of the city, he stops and, hidden from sight, takes a handful of dried grass, whose smell evokes the country. He puts it in his pocket and, with tears in his eyes, climbs back into the truck to begin his new life.

The analysis of the problem from the perspective of the individual removes it from the realm of statistics and imbues it with great emotional quality. Miss Medio emphasizes the dilemma of families like this one ; the opportunity of the promised land of the city is contrasted with the pull of tradition and the past, represented by emotional ties to the land of one's fathers. She also widens the scope by referring to others who have made or are making the same move, inferring that Marín's problem must be multiplied many times to get the true picture of Spain's shifting structures today.

IV   *Fictional Sketches*

Four short pieces have appeared in recent issues of *QP*, the National Telephone Company magazine. Their extreme brevity— two pages allotted to each—provides only enough room for a sketch, but this is ample space to develop a situation with a maximum of emotional impact.[5] "Cinco cartas de Alemania" ("Five Letters from Germany") presents still another social reality with a wry comment on the fickleness of human nature.[6] The problem of the emigré, especially those who go to Germany to make their fortune, has been the result of the uneven Spanish economy. In "Five Letters . . . ," Eugenia anxiously awaits a letter from her son who has gone to Germany and who only writes sporadically. Mariana, a neighbor and Pablo's childhood sweetheart, reads the letters to Eugenia, and the two daydream about their happy lives when Pablo returns. The younger woman spends time talking to and cheering up Eugenia, who in turn considers her already as her daughter-in-law. When Pablo does return, however, he brings an unexpected present: his German wife and their baby. The new grandmother is so thrilled with her "surprise" that she neither notices Mariana's sudden disappearance, in her new-found pleasure, nor thinks of the younger girl's grief.

"El cochecito de Miguelín"[7] ("Little Miguel's Baby Carriage") provides another unhappy ending. An old woman adored her paralytic grandson and would wheel him around Madrid in his carriage. After his death, she refused to get rid of the carriage, and now uses it as a portable stand from which she sells candy and comics on the street. One day a car knocks her down and completely ruins the carriage, thus destroying the material symbol of the baby and her love for him.

"Teresa (Solo de recuerdos para un hombre)" ("Teresa, a Solo Composed of Memories for a Man") is a telephone monologue.[8] A man calls his former sweetheart on the telephone and explains at length the reasons for his long delay in setting a marriage date: the necessity for economic security, the Civil War, later ambitions for wealth, other meaningless affairs. He contrasts the woman's idea that love should be the only important factor in life and her arguments that his own reasoning was a mask for selfishness and cowardice. Although it is now too late for children, he has returned to her. He comments on the laughter or sobs he hears on the phone, but the listener never talks. Suddenly the phone goes dead, and the man cannot get the connection again. He learns from the operator that the number has been out of service since the woman who owned it died a week ago.

"Milagro en Santaolaya" ("Miracle in Santaolaya") concerns Pasca, an older woman, whose fanciful and absent-minded behavior has not affected her basic goodness: she is constantly helping the people in the town.[9] Her greatest eccentricity is to care for a doll her fiancé had won for her at a fair; after he deserted her, she treated it like a real baby. One day the town learns that a real baby was found in Pasca's house; the story of the miraculous change soon brings the village priest, who is rather dubious about the authenticity of the miracle. Doña Pasca reminds him that there are also miracles that save a woman's honor. Later the reader learns that doña Pasca does consider the child a miracle: first, she now has an heir for her estate and someone to love; secondly, she is saving the honor of a married woman whose husband was in Germany and obviously could not be the father of the child.

These four stories deal in some way with love and, with the exception of the "miracle" and its quasi-happy ending, Miss Medio describes the pain that love can cause, the egoism and selfishness of human behavior, the lack of communication even between lovers, man's loneliness, and especially the hurt caused by separation— whether death, temporary absence, or desertion.

V   *General Characteristics*

An overview of the short fiction during this period reveals a thread of common concern which binds the disparate works together. In theme and subject matter, much allies them to the nonautobiographical novels: the preference for characters from the middle and lower classes, and for unfortunate individuals living in physical and spiritual misery. A rough outline of the outstanding elements must include the description of poverty and the various attempts (mostly failures) to overcome it; shattered dreams, hopes, or ideals; brusque intrusion of reality; lack of communication or understanding; the author's constant awareness of the way structures mold, change, and determine the individual life.

Some hidden law seems to prevent the characters from solving their problems, from gaining their ideal. They may be victims of an abstract "system," but it is even more evident that man's worst enemy is man. With few exceptions ("The Miracle in Santaolaya" comes to mind immediately), each is so engrossed in his own affairs that he cannot help others; indeed, he may take advantage of his fellowman.

Miss Medio refrains from intervention in these works. She simply presents a situation so manifestly unjust that there can be no room for doubt, and lets the facts speak for themselves. Her only means of commentary is through pathos and irony, modes which are generally present throughout the stories and arise from situations which become patterns through repetition.

CHAPTER 10

Miscellaneous Works

A side from copious newspaper production, Miss Medio has also written several book-length works which do not fall into the realm of novel or short stories. Yet even these disparate works reveal a constancy of outlook which, given her approach to literature, is not surprising in itself, but which adds an unusual tone to the nonfictional books. The preference for the personal instead of the factual, the interest in the individual and the sympathy which was noticeable in her novels spills over into a literature in which author intrusion is usually at a minimum, if not completely and necessarily absent.

I A Book for Children

El Milagro de la Noche de Reyes (The Miracle of Epiphany Eve) centers around an exciting moment for the Spanish child: the time when the Three Kings bring presents to good children.[1] The story describes the arrival of the Three Kings, their entrance into a toy store where the Dream Fairy regales them and the children with stories about the Star on the Christmas tree, how a naughty princess was changed into a doll, the adventures of a toy gnome, and many other sketches. Dawn arrives and the toys described are presented to the children; snow comes to erase the last trace of the Kings' cavalcade.

As she wrote this work, Miss Medio was doubtless thinking of the young students she had known, for it is told from the point of view of a child. The vocabulary is very simple; personification abounds (the sun, the star on the tree, the snow), the reactions and lessons learned are based on simple concepts. The characters are ones with which her young audience would already be quite familiar (Puss in Boots, Mickey Mouse, Little Red Riding Hood), although she purposely changes some of the adventures. The book offers pleasant reading for the child, and often teaches a lesson as well.

II   *Biographical Works*

Under a grant from the Fundación March, Miss Medio was commissioned to do a work for a series on important Spaniards. In 1966 the results were published: the biography of Isabel II, Queen of Spain from 1833 until her exile in 1868.[2] In general, history has not been kind to this queen, who was forced into an undesirable marriage and into a political system for which she obviously was not suited. Her reign was marked by instability in both public and private life: paralleling the turnover of ministers and governments, formed and dissolved with amazing rapidity, was a series of personal favorites and lovers which made Isabel II the scandal of Spain and Europe.

A glance at some of the history books reveals the image she has left for posterity. Words like *frivolous, incompetent, ignorant,* are mild compared to some of the more detailed accounts of her life. One historian says of her reign that it was "a continuous struggle between her own instinct (and the desire of her court) to rule autocratically and the increasing demand of the Spanish people for honest and efficient government . . . It was a quarter of a century of kaleidoscopic political change, revolution, constitutional amendments—and misrule."[3] Another comments on her scandalous behavior: "In private life she created her own standards of behavior. In public life she conformed to the traditions of her worthy parents. She betrayed her first prime minister."[4]

Miss Medio, in a brief prologue, explains the difficulty of the biographer who strives for objectivity, yet may not be able to create a complete dimension of truth because of necessary selection of details. For this reason, the author states emphatically that she will report not only some of the more unfavorable aspects of Isabel's life, but her good points as well, which were not always evident "because of the slyness and cunning of the politicians who surrounded her" (p. 10).

Miss Medio tackles the question of historical biography from a personal point of view. She tries to give the human side of history whenever she can—the reactions of the people, the human factors which determine decisions and policies, the interests of the people at the court and how they, in turn, influenced the Queen. This technique adds another dimension to the usual objective historical approach, giving the biography the air of a historical novel. Miss

Medio's characterization of Isabel's mother, María Cristina, is an excellent example of the personal approach to history: she had married secretly after King Ferdinand's death, and was trying to conceal the fact that she was pregnant: " . . . the first fruits of this marriage put the august lady on the spot: pains, nausea, fainting, she had to hide it all and smile, smile at the people, who had to be ignorant of this secret marriage, incompatible with her position as ruler of the kingdom, as widow of Ferdinand VII and guardian of the child Queen." (pp. 33–34) Miss Medio has established a tension between the duties of the government and human desires, a problem which was to beset Isabel as well. In this case, Miss Medio investigates why María Cristina would have married three months after Ferdinand's death, since such a union was invalid before the law. She ascribes the reason to María Cristina's temperament, which overshadowed her education : she was a passionate person and could not live without a man. This conjecture gives depth to an otherwise colorless, rather disagreeable woman. Yet Miss Medio, always attuned to the effects of heredity and environment on her "character," whether real or fictional, obviously believes that a set of circumstances had forced María Cristina—and later Isabel—into a role which was distasteful to her and to which she was unsuited. In case there may be any question on this point, the author states her ideas on development in the first pages of the biography: "Two primordial causes determine the personality of the individual: heredity and the environment or circumstances which modify it [the personality]" (p. 11).

When describing the Queen's more unfortunate attributes, Miss Medio tries to give a logical excuse for them or focus on Isabel's possible reactions to her deficient upbringing. For example, she reports on the young Queen's lack of interest in her studies, and goes on to conjecture, "But did anyone make an effort to make the work pleasant for her, to try to interest her in the material she had to know, and to instruct her, by conviction, in her duties as Queen? Possibly not" (p.71). Once again, the author discusses the problem of education from the student's point of view, and by extension, royal duties through the eyes of one who became the victim of an elaborate system. She also presents a convincing case that many of the mistakes made by Isabel—both serious and trivial—were due to a combination of bad advice and her intuitive and emotional approach to government: "The uncertainty that the people who

surrounded her sowed in the mind of the little queen, concerning
good and evil, concerning her duties as woman and sovereign, and
concerning what was or was not suitable for the country, was later
to be the characteristic note of her private life and kingdom" (p. 81).

Even though she has promised to be objective, Miss Medio resorts
to a favorite metaphor: life as a theater or a circus, here particularly
appropriate since she has repeatedly showed that Isabel was forced
to play a role which was completely foreign to her character and
temperament. One example is the Queen's unhappiness at having
to marry without love, a feeling she must hide from her subjects:
"But it was necessary to smile from the royal box, like the clowns
in the circus. An entire nation was watching her. Her people.
Before whom she had to show herself 'a queen,' hiding her womanly
feelings" (p. 119). The role-playing, stressed before and later, makes
clear that the real Isabel—the woman—had to be overshadowed by
her role, that of queen. Thus the words that evoke the theatrical
theme—*drama, comedy, tragedy, spectator,* etc.—are used with
deliberate intention to emphasize Isabel's dual existence.

Isabel's notorious reputation was due to a large number of ill-
concealed love affairs. Miss Medio discusses this point, but is quick
to defend the Queen through her theory of the formation of the
personality: environment and heredity, the same factors to which
she attributed Isabel's poor government.

Were it only the circumstances which surrounded her that determined
her desperate anxiety to live and love, one could imagine that Isabel II,
married like her sister Luisa Fernanda to a virile and energetic man, would
have been a good wife. It can also be admitted that, given her bland and
malleable character, her docility and, especially, her good heart, qualities
of which she had given constant proof, if from childhood she had been
surrounded by honest and sincere persons, who were interested above all
things in the good government of the country, her reign would have been
excellent. But we cannot disregard heredity, which with its blind force
generally determines the lives of people. Her grandmother . . . and great-
grandmother . . . suffered certain erotic disturbances, aggravated in Isabel
II by an itching skin condition. If to this we add her ill-directed education,
her deficient training, and in a very special way, the lack of scruples in
the people who would influence her powerfully, the result should not
surprise anyone." (pp. 141–42)

Miss Medio has presented the historical framework tempered by
a sympathetic compassion toward her subject. She does not gloss

over the fact that Isabel was a dreadful ruler, utterly unsuited even for the task of figurehead of State. But she does alternate these facts with the human side of the Queen. Lost in a world of intrigue to which she was not equal, rather childlike in spite of her years, unable to see the consequences of her actions, unhappily married to a man who was probably impotent, Isabel was obviously divided in her loyalties to her country and her personal interests. To mitigate the impression of such frivolity, the author has selected and put forth determinants which may have caused Isabel to act the way she did, a method designed to elicit understanding and pity on the part of the reader. Once again the novelist has tried to find the common factor, which she applies to the highest ranking person as well as to a character from the lowest class : their importance as human beings, which must take precedence over class, history, or abstract ideas.

A second biography appeared in 1971. The novelist turned from Spanish royalty to one of her own profession, Selma Lagerlöf (1858–1940), the Swedish recipient of the Nobel Prize for literature in 1909.[5] Miss Lagerlöf was born in the province of Värmland, well known for its dramatic scenery and, in days before her childhood, for its sumptuous style of life. Her most famous books recreate stories and legends of her beloved Värmland (*The Saga of Gosta Borling* [1891], *Invisible Links* [1894]); the more realistic *Jerusalem* (2 vols., 1901–1902), describes a group of Swedish farmers who emigrated to Palestine.

The work is a short biography-*cum*-anthology in which Miss Medio explores the few intimate details available and speculates about the lack of seemingly indispensable information concerning Miss Lagerlöf's emotional life. Miss Medio stated that her real interest in the Swedish writer dated from the time she was working on the biography. Surely she must have noticed and felt the affinities which are immediately apparent in the lives of the two women: Aside from the obvious fact that both are women writers, both were teachers who later turned writer, both wrote a book for children, both spent their childhood in regions known for their spectacular beauty, both rocketed to fame through a single work. Although their literature differs radically in content, some of Miss Lagerlöf's novels have some social concern and a more realistic approach, which would parallel her biographer's own interests.

As usual, Miss Medio prefers to explore the formative influences which are apparent in Miss Lagerlöf's works; thus she stresses the fantasy awakened in the little girl through the tales and legends told by her grandmother and the other old women of the region. Miss Medio's interest in heredity and environment leads her to point to outstanding characteristics in the literature—the fantastic elements, the pervading religious concern, the love of nature— which are direct products of childhood upbringing.

With little concrete data to work from, Miss Medio uses factual material, then reconstructs probable events in her subject's life. She seems greatly disturbed by the lack of information concerning love interest, and so turns to Selma Lagerlöf's works in order to reconstruct possible emotional affinities between the heroines and their creator, inferring parallels between Miss Lagerlöf's techniques and her own.

For those more interested in Miss Medio's attitudes, there are several interesting "asides" which she interjects into the work: comments on the profession of the novelist, of the teacher, the likes and dislikes of children, and other topics which move away from strict biography into the realm of personal commentary.

III   *A Regional Guidebook*

Under another grant from the March Foundation, Miss Medio turned her hand to an entirely different type of book : a guide of Asturias,[6] part of a collection of guides to Spain sponsored by the publishing company Destino. As a native of Asturias, Miss Medio was the perfect choice to present this section to both the initiated and the uninitiated, for she supplements her research and knowledge with a love of the region which shows through the most objective descriptions. The huge six-hundred-page tome is filled with many excellent black-and-white photographs which illustrate the points of special interest.

Although such a work could easily lend itself to dry facts and endless lists of local wonders, Miss Medio again adapts her own philosophy of writing to the task, and the guidebook is all the better for it. More than a simple geographical description of the sites of local interest, Asturias through Miss Medio's eyes has depth in its multifaceted role as historical site, tourist attraction, the marriage of progress and tradition, and most of all, a place inhabited by people and of interest to people.

She enriches the facts with literary allusions, quoting from notables from the region or referring to works set in Asturias. Thus she mentions Ortega y Gasset, Jovellanos, Clarín, Pérez de Ayala, Palacio Valdés, and Casona, among others, adding a dimension which would make the trip to Asturias a literary pilgrimage.

For those less intellectually inclined, she enumerates the abundant sports, breathtaking scenery, and then personalizes the spot by interjecting anecdotes, local traditions, legends, superstitions, local sayings, popular poetry—in short, anything that presents human existence in relation with the region.

She is excellent at the recreation of scenes from everyday life, using her artist's eye and pen to convey the overall impression to the reader. A description of the old section of Oviedo, Cimadevilla, reads,

> Old streets and old buildings, convents, ancestral houses and humble fisherman's dwellings, mingling in affable neighborliness and friendship. . . Mansions run-down, but still standing, hold up with dignity the humble shacks which in former times sought protection from them . . . Clothing hung out in the wind, that sea wind that blows and blows, as if playing hide-and-go-seek along the narrow, damp alleys of Cimadevilla. The siren of a boat which enters the port. The strong smell of the succulent dishes from the taverns. Children who play half naked, tanned by the sea air . . . A strong manly voice breaks the silence suddenly, with echoes of a sea conch and a harsh mountain sound." (p. 131)

One note sustained throughout the work is the continual emphasis on the difference between the old and the new parts of Asturias, with special emphasis on contrast within a single city or region. She is well aware of the problems that industrialization has brought this region, although she is quick to point out the good and bad points of each. Yet there is obviously a nostalgic preference for tradition, and a feeling for the old Spain which is rapidly and inexorably being supplanted by its modern counterpart. A village which had to be flooded for a modern dam is considered a victim of progress : she calls the works a "modern dragon" which devoured "several villages, an endless amount of houses, farm land and memories of old peasants, who were obliged to join in the new life which new times impose" (p. 475). This kind of commentary, a more "objective" transmutation of a similar one in the short story "Giddy-up, Nicolasa," shows the continuing interest in social themes.

The choice of photographs reinforces the philosophy of the work, alternating views of the countryside with those of people and their activities: wash drying in the sun, wooden shoes outside the door of a palace, women washing under the most primitive conditions with a ninth-century tower in the background, perhaps a silent commentary that things have not changed so radically.

IV *Poetry*

Miss Medio's creative talents have been recognized in the area of prose fiction, but she has also steadily written poetry of which very little has been published. She has supplied me with typed copies of several poems, but could not remember if they had been published or not. She also intimated that there were many more scattered about and that she was planning to publish a collection of miscellaneous poetry in the near future.[7]

The subject matter varies greatly : some of the pieces are children's poetry composed when she was a teacher. Others treat more serious subjects : the paradox of love, with its welcome pain ; memories of her street in Oviedo. One composition doubtless was the progenitor of "Shall We Go, Timoteo?" (*Andrés*), for it describes an under-privileged child who equates life with a circus. "El ataúd" ("The Coffin"), 1936, describes her mother's coffin, fashioned from a box which originally contained soap (one of the few sources of wood available during the Civil War, when coffins were at a premium); the coffin has lettering and a blue bird painted on it. Other works describe intensely personal feelings and reactions ("I will Die Alone," "Anguish," "Silence"). Many of the poems are quite bitter in tone, pointing to the ironies of life or death, the solitude of the individual, the inequality of humanity.

CHAPTER 11

Summary and Conclusions

A survey of Miss Medio's complete literary production reveals some variation in form from the first work to the present, but the differences in style have simply reinforced consistent literary ideas which indicate a coherent philosophical whole. This permits some generalization about the more than one dozen published works and over twenty-five years of steady writing (fiction, nonfictional books, newspaper articles).

Two major groupings divide the body of her work, each distinguished by similar attributes in the leading character. One group presents a female figure reminiscent of the author herself. This person is young, observant, solitary, and given to comments about life. Her psychological (and at times physical) distance from the action is enough to permit her to comment on it, and even scrutinize her own feelings with some degree of objectivity. These novels are patently autobiographical in character, and the women's analytical tendencies permit a freer expression of the author's own views on the subject under consideration. Such works include *We Riveros,* portions of *The Fish Stays Afloat,* and *Diary of a Schoolteacher.*

The second group, by far the more numerous, develops a character who is simultaneously important as an individual and as a representative of a large group, generally the middle or lower class. No distinguishing features or outstanding traits differentiate these people from the thousands like them; their very averageness is the quality that Miss Medio seeks. This group includes *Public Servant,* portions of *The Fish Stays Afloat, Bibiana,* and the short stories.

Both categories present a similar pattern in which the characters face "tests" of different kinds, be they in the form of social or psychological pressures, or a specific crisis like a mine disaster. The females of the autobiographical works generally undergo a traumatic experience which is almost an initiation rite: it forces them to take a decisive step in their lives and move into a new era, generally one of responsibility to others (selflessness, or ethical duties), at which time they mature and accept independence. The other characters generally do not enjoy this outcome; the situation may bring their lives into the spotlight for the moment, but they soon realize that despite the effort, their condition is unalterable (Mr. García; Jenara of *Tomorrow*).

Solitude is another quality that most characters share; married couples are no exception to this unhappy rule. They suffer from alienation from the social order (inability to adjust or open rebellion and refusal to conform); on the personal level there is a notable lack of understanding, the inability to communicate on anything but the most elementary level, a lack of good faith, and the impossibility of opening oneself to an honest relationship. There are cases of "false" friendship, in which only self-interest is the motivating factor (the office staff with Mr. García; the American lady with the bellboy in *Andrés*); others ignore a call for help because involvement might be bothersome (Bibiana and Eladia). Often one will refuse to recognize the true qualities of another, preferring a more idealized image. Apparently the only answer to this problem is self-reliance and an inner strength which would allow one to accept what comes with equanimity; however, this is only the case within the autobiographical works.

This provides the reader with the idea of how self-sufficient the women must be, for they can rely on no one but themselves; those who do (Lena Rivero, Veva Martínez [*The Fish* . . .], and Irene Gal) are most successful, within limits; those who have depended on another and have not taken the step to freedom suffer for it, an interesting (and perhaps unconscious) psychological commentary on human nature and the consequences of a strong relationship.

Consistent patterns are also in evidence throughout Miss Medio's work. Many characters construct the very substance of their own lives on a certain image which is more imaginary than real. Max, Natalia Blay, Gina Planell, the American woman (*Andrés*) are examples of the ideal person; the characters endow them with qualities that have no connection with reality. The Second Republic, a new life, a better job, a raise, the lottery are examples of more intangible but no less important dreams. Invariably, these ideals are shattered at the end of the work, although the effects of such disappointment are generally understated (thus making the pathos even more touching). In the autobiographical works, the disappointment simply serves as a proving ground for the inner strength of the character, but in other works it may shatter the character completely (García, Jenara).

A certain environmental determinism conditions the lives of the characters, who remain in the same position with no possibility of change. Even under the illusion of freedom of action, a counterforce ironically points to the futility of such intentions. The family, society, or group pressure may provide the environmental factor, or conditions like hardship or poverty may offer the motivation for action. The clearest expression is in *Tomorrow*, but *We Riveros* even presents the idea in its theoretical form. The suggestion is even hinted at in the last novel, where Miss Medio insinuates that Bibiana has been conditioned to be what she is and cannot change; the non-fictional biographical works also approach the subject from this point of view.

Man's place in society is a central issue in these books. Although the characters may rebel against the existing social order, they eventually conform (Pablo, Jenara), a predictable move given Miss Medio's theory of the necessity to adapt to the social environment. The individual, however, may become an unsuspecting and un-protesting "victim" of a system which permits taking advantage of the weak (*Andrés* is the outstanding example of this because of the symbolic helplessness of the children). The author also questions meaningless or outmoded values, especially artificial ones estab-lished by the middle class, whose only aim is to keep up appearances (Mrs. Rivero, for example).

Patterns of contemporary life are measured through personal reaction and the effect that wide-sweeping political or social changes would have on the individual. Emigration, rapid mechanization, big business and its inevitable dehumanization, the sudden acqui-sition of wealth are all subthemes of the individual's relationship with society. Rapid changes cause a sense of unease and insecurity: "Giddy-up, Nicolasa" or "A Handful of Dry Grass" bears witness to the nostalgia and pain with which the characters leave the old ways behind.

The style with which Miss Medio presents these ideas is basically simple and realistic. Her prose is deliberately clear and concise, so that the reader can easily follow the train of thought. There is also some experimentation in form whenever it can be used to best advantage: interior monologue allows for the withdrawal of author intervention; popular speech, thought patterns, and extensive use of dialogue give the main emphasis to the character and allow the reader to form his own conclusions. Miss Medio often creates a situation which forces the reader to abandon his omniscient perspective, placing him on the level of the character.

The novelist is very aware of the responsibility of the artist vis-à-vis his public, since the work of art is a perfect teaching situation. Although she does not believe in the novel as a deliberate means of propaganda, her obvious sympathy for the characters and the elucidation of problems inherent in the classes which she describes create an awareness of inequities which need to be remedied. At the very least it is a call for solidarity through mutual suffering, understanding, and love.

Although it is entirely possible that Miss Medio will change her style and even modify essential themes, we may predict that her abiding interest in the ordinary person and his relationship with the contemporary social structure will continue to be a major concern in her literature and her personal philosophy.

Notes and References

Chapter One

1. For the interested student, a partial list of books published on the contemporary Spanish novel would include Juan Luis Alborg, *Hora actual de la novela española,* 2 vols. (Madrid: Taurus, 1958); Rafael Bosch, *La novela española del siglo XX,* II (New York: Las Américas, 1970); Ramón Buckley, *Problemas formales en la novela española contemporánea* (Barcelona: Ediciones Península, 1968); Juan Carlos Curutchet, *Introducción a la novela española de postguerra* (Montevideo: Editorial Alfa, 1966); M. García Viñó, *Novela española actual* (Madrid: Guadarrama, 1967); Edenia Guillermo and Juana Amelia Hernández, *La novelística española de los 60* (New York: Eliseo Torres and Sons, 1971); Pablo Gil Casado, *La novela social española* (Barcelona, Seix Barral, 1968); Antonio Iglesias Laguna, *Treinta años de novela española* (Madrid: Editorial Prensa Española, 1969); Eugenio G. de Nora, *La novela española contemporánea,* II, ii (Madrid: Gredos, 1962); Rodrigo Rubio, *Narrativa española, 1940–1970* (Madrid: E.P.E.S.A., 1970); Gonzalo Sobejano, *Novela española de nuestro tiempo* (Madrid: Editorial Prensa Española, 1970).

2. García Viñó, *op. cit.* p. 111.

3. Ana María Matute, untitled article, trans. by William Fifield, in the *Kenyon Review,* XXXI, 126 (1969), 453.

Chapter Two

1. Unless otherwise noted, the information in this chapter comes from the following sources: interviews by this writer with Miss Medio (June, 1970 and June, 1972); correspondence between this writer and Miss Medio, dated March 5, 1971 and January 25, 1972; a printed Curriculum Vitae prepared by the novelist for distribution; and the following article: Janet Winecoff, "Fictionalized Autobiography in the Novels of Dolores Medio," *Kentucky Foreign Language Quarterly,* 13, No. 3 (1966), 170–78.

2. Interview, June, 1972.

3. Letter from Miss Medio dated January 25, 1972.

4. Joaquín Arrarás, *Historia de la segunda república española* (Madrid: Editora Nacional, 1964), II, 531–654.

5. Interview, June, 1972.

6. *Ibid.*

7. *Ibid.*

8. Rafael Vázquez-Zamora, "Dolores Medio. De *Nosotros los Rivero* a Ellas, las de la 'Celda común,'" *Destino* (October 15, 1966), p. 63.

9. In the United States, *Funcionario público* is now available in a classroom edition by Oxford University Press; Terrell Tatum's edition of *Cuentos recientes de España* (New York: Charles Scribner's Sons, 1960) contains two short stories and a chapter from *Nosotros los Rivero*.

10. Dolores Medio, untitled lecture in *El autor enjuicia su obra* (Madrid: Editora Nacional, 1966), p. 157. Brackets around suspensive points indicate material that I have omitted from the original quotation.

11. *Ibid.,* p. 156.

12. *Ibid.,* p. 158.

13. *Ibid.,* p. 163.

14. *Ibid.,* p. 165.

15. Dolores Medio, "Curriculum Vitae."

16. Dolores Medio, *Discurso* (Santander: Aldus Velarde, 1967), p. 9.

17. Letter from Miss Medio dated March, 1971.

18. Miguel de Unamuno, *En torno al casticismo*, 4th ed. (Madrid: Espasa Calpe, 1957), pp. 27–28.

19. José Ortega y Gasset, "Azorín: primores de lo vulgar," *El espectador,* in *Obras completas*, 7th ed. (Madrid: Revista de Occidente, 1966) II, 186.

20. Interview, June, 1972.

21. *Ibid.*

22. "La otra circunstancia" which Miss Medio described in the June, 1972 interview.

23. Dolores Medio, *Discurso*, p. 8.

24. Dolores Medio, "La lectura forma parte de la educación," *Arriba* (April 11, 1965), p. 26.

25. Dolores Medio, *Discurso*, p. 8.

26. *Ibid.*

27. Answer to a questionnaire submitted by this author in a letter from Miss Medio dated March 5, 1971.

28. Dolores Medio, Untitled lecture in *El autor enjuicia su obra*, p. 161.

29. *Ibid.*

30. Dolores Medio, *Discurso*, p. 7.

Chapter Three

1. Dolores Medio, "Nina," *Cuentistas españolas contemporáneas* (Madrid: Aguilar, 1946), pp. 375–92.

2. Dolores Medio, *Compás de espera* (Barcelona: Ediciones G.P., 1954).

3. Janet Winecoff, "Fictionalized Autobiography in the Novels of Dolores Medio," *Kentucky For. Lang. Quarterly,* 13, 170–78, has noted the importance of economic problems in Miss Medio's works.

4. Dolores Medio, *Mañana, Cinco novelas, La novela del sábado,* II, 67 (Madrid: Ediciones Cid, 1954).

5. Dolores Medio, "Patio de luces," *El Español,* No. 291 (June 27–July 3, 1954), pp. 36–42.

Chapter Four

1. Dolores Medio, *Nosotros los Rivero.* Ours is the 7th ed. (Barcelona: Destino, 1958).

2. Miss Medio has stated that much of this novel is based on her personal experience; people she has known also formed the basis for many characters. The biographical material will show the coincidence of facts between the author and her character. This aspect has been treated in Janet Winecoff, "Fictionalized Autobiography in the Novels of Dolores Medio," *Kentucky For. Lang. Quarterly,* 13, 170–78. Some other points of coincidence not touched on in the article are Heidi's running away, El Aguilucho's mysterious letter, the visit by the Prince of Asturias.

3. Interview with Miss Medio, June, 1972.

4. Antonio de Hoyos, *Ocho escritores actuales* (Murcia: Aula de Cultura, 1954), pp. 231–32.

5. These are selected excerpts from two articles, but could be multiplied: M. Arroita-Jáuregui, review of *Nosotros los Rivero, Correo literario* (May 15, 1953), n.p.; Celso Collazo, "El Nadal de este año," *Pueblo* (May 5, 1953), n.p.

6. Enrique Sordo, "Notas al margen: *Nosotros los Rivero,*" *Revista Gran Vía de actualidades, artes y letras* (April 30, 1953), p. 11.

7. Antonio de Hoyos, *op. cit.,* p. 233.

8. Rafael Vázquez Zamora, "*Funcionario público* de Dolores Medio," *Destino* (March, 1957), p. 32.

9. Janet Winecoff, "Fictionalized Autobiography . . . ," *op. cit.,* p. 171.

10. Fernando Ponce, "Dolores Medio en la novela de hoy," *Punta Europa* (November, 1967), p. 58.

11. Letter from Miss Medio dated March 5, 1971. See Chapter 2, p. 32 for part of this quotation.

12. This device is well known in Pérez Galdós' series of novels dealing with Spain's history, the *Episodios nacionales,* which immerse the lives of ordinary characters in a specific historical moment, thus affecting the course of their existence. More modern authors have also adopted the same procedure: Miguel de Unamuno, *Paz in la guerra* (1897) and Ignacio Agustí in *Mariona Rebull* (1944). The last two, which are also first novels, are affiliated more with the Realistic mode of writing.

13. Letter from Miss Medio dated March 5, 1961.

14. Arroita Jáuregui, *op. cit.;* also a review in *Juventud* (May 13, 1953, no author, n.p.) states that it is a "bad translation of any cheap North American novel."

15. M. Reyero Riaño, "Dolores Medio, alumna de la escuela superior de educación de la F.A.E., Premio Nadal 1952,"*Atenas* (February, 1953), p. 31.

16. One critic, for example, says of the "curse": "The 'black butterflies' which afflict Lena so much are simply hysteria; . . . the legend of the Riveros is a sensational device which plays too outstanding a role in the story, in spite of the fact that it never convinces the reader effectively." J. Mª M. C., Review of *Nosotros los Rivero, Boletín del Instituto de Estudios Asturianos*, VI, No. 20 (1953), 615–17.

17. Galdós often expounded on the differences between history and what he called "internal history."

Chapter Five

1. Dolores Medio, *Funcionario público* (Barcelona: Destino, 1956).

2. This is no doubt an echo of the author's own concern about the mercenary attitudes of postwar Madrid. She has commented with disillusionment about the struggle for survival and the demoralization it causes in honest people (Interview, June, 1972).

3. Dolores Medio, *Discurso*, p. 20.

4. A. Valencia, *"Funcionario público,"* *Arriba* (January 10, 1957), p. 15.

5. Rafael Vázquez Zamora, *"Funcionario público* de Dolores Medio," *Destino* (March, 1957), p. 32.

6. Interview of June, 1970.

7. Letter from Miss Medio dated January 25, 1972.

Chapter Six

1. Dolores Medio, *El pez sigue flotando* (Barcelona: Destino, 1959).

2. Many of her characters have already appeared in Miss Medio's works: from "Inner Courtyard" comes the story of Morales and Gina; "El cuadro" is condensed into the episode with Dr. Brau and Mme Garín; "Unpunished Crime" is also repeated (See Chapter 2). Lena Rivero, of course, had been introduced in *We Riveros*, but her adventures in this novel have not been alluded to before.

3. Eugenio G. de Nora, *La novela española contemporánea* (Madrid: Gredos, 1962), II, ii, 120.

4. José Ortega y Gasset, "El tema de nuestro tiempo," *Obras completas*, 6th ed. (Madrid: Revista de Occidente, 1966), III, 199.

5. In her letter of January 25, 1972, the author wrote the following in answer to a questionnaire: "Yes, I knew Ortega y Gasset personally, but I was not a pupil of his. . . .My fiancé, the great love of my life, the man who had so much influence on my education, was a pupil of his, and in turn was my best teacher. For many years I identified with his ideas, until I began to cultivate my own thoughts, and I began to differ in some

aspects with Ortega, but all in all, my admiration for Ortega remains firm and I continuously read his works, where I always find something wonderful. His thought does not always convince me, but what always enchants me is his clear prose, his form of placing things within the reach of everyone with a clarity and beauty that seduces. It is difficult to point out which book . . . has influenced me most. Perhaps because it is the first one I read, I almost memorized "The Spectator," but I reread his *Complete Works* constantly." See Chapter Two for further comments on Ortega.

6. Another point of contact with *Public Servant*.

Chapter Seven

1. Dolores Medio, *Diario de una maestra* (Barcelona: Destino, 1961).

2. Letter from Miss Medio dated January 25, 1972.

3. Juan Luis Alborg, *Hora actual de la novela española* (Madrid: Taurus, 1962), II, 345–46.

4. Letter from Miss Medio dated January 25, 1972.

5. A. Valencia, "El idealismo en Dolores Medio," *Arriba* (April 26, 1961), p. 17.

6. Dolores Medio, "Psicología y técnica del cuento infantil," *Arriba* (November 17, 1963), p. 20.

7. The series is entitled "Literatura juvenil," and appeared in four parts in *Arriba* on the following dates: April 10, 1966 (p. 23); April 17, 1966 (p. 26); April 21, 1966 (p. 24); April 28, 1966 (p. 21).

8. From a three-part article in *Arriba* entitled "Algo sobre el cine infantil," published on the following dates: November 24, 1963 (pp. 15–16); December 8, 1963 (p. 18); February 2, 1964 (p. 20).

9. Dolores Medio, "Benavente y la educación," *Arriba* (April 12, 1964), p. 22.

10. Dolores Medio, "Aquel hermoso 'Lepintan,'" *Arriba* (January 6, 1965), p. 22.

11. Alborg, *op. cit.*, p. 17.

12. Helen Parkhurst, *Education on the Dalton Plan* (London: G. Bell and Sons, Ltd., 1922), pp. 24–25.

Chapter Eight

1. *Bibiana* was first published in 1963 (Madrid: Ed. Bullón). References in this text are taken from the 1967 edition printed by Ediciones Destino.

2. In a letter expressing indignation about "what should always be concealed," he continues, "Does she believe that her book could be put in the hands of the youth? Would she leave it within reach of her former pupils, or any unmarried person? What does the work gain with such scabrousness?" Marcelino del Real, "Carta a Dolores Medio," *Maestro* (February 1964), n.p.

3. Luis López Anglada, "El autor y su obra: *Bibiana*," *El Español* (February 15, 1964), n.p.

4. Among others Manuel Cerezales, "Libros: *Bibiana*," *El Alcázar* (November 20, 1967), n.p., and Janet Winecoff, "Fictionalized Autobiography in the Novels of Dolores Medio," p. 174.

Chapter Nine

1. Dolores Medio, *El señor García*, La novela popular, No. 33 (Madrid: Alfaguara, 1966).

2. Dolores Medio, *Andrés* (Oviedo: Richard Grandio, 1967).

3. Dolores Medio, "Tira, Nicolasa . . . !," *Punta Europa*, No. 127 (November, 1967), pp. 69–75.

4. Dolores Medio, "El puñado de yerba seca," *Informaciones* (April 24, 1969), p. 8.

5. These sketches are to be the kernels for longer works. Miss Medio has stated her intention of revising and expanding them at a later date (Interview, June, 1972).

6. Dolores Medio, "Cinco cartas de Alemania," *QP: Revista para los empleados de la Compañía Telefónica* (April, 1967), pp. 10–12.

7. Dolores Medio, "El cochecito de Miguelín," *QP: Revista para los empleados de la Compañía Telefónica* (July, 1970), pp. 10–12.

8. Dolores Medio, "Teresa (Solo de recuerdos para un hombre)," *QP: Revista para los empleados de la Compañía Telefónica* (October, 1970), pp. 10–12.

9. Dolores Medio, "Milagro en Santaolaya," *QP: Revista para los empleados de la Compañía Telefónica* (September, 1971), pp. 10–12.

Chapter Ten

1. Dolores Medio, *El milagro de la Noche de Reyes*, 3rd ed. 1948 (rpt. Burgos: Hijos de Santiago Rodríguez, 1958).

2. Dolores Medio, *Isabel II de España* (Madrid: Editorial Sucesores de Rivadeneyra, 1966).

3. Rafael Altamira, *A History of Spain*, trans. from 2nd ed. by Muna Lee, 1949 (rpt. Toronto-New York-London: D. Van Nostand Co., Inc., 1958), p. 560.

4. Salvador de Madariaga, *Spain: A Modern History*, 2nd ed. (New York: Frederick A. Praeger, 1960), p. 63.

5. Dolores Medio, *Selma Lagerlöf* (Madrid: E.P.E.S.A., 1971).

6. Dolores Medio, *Asturias* (Barcelona: Ediciones Destino, 1971).

7. I have listed the poetry in my possession in the bibliographical works of Miss Medio under "Poetry."

Selected Bibliography

(See Notes and References for further bibliographical orientation.)

Primary Sources

1. The Works of Dolores Medio

A. Novels

Bibiana (Madrid: Ed. Bullón, 1963) Also Barcelona: Ediciones Destino, 1967).

Diario de una maestra (Barcelona: Ediciones Destino, 1961).

Funcionario público (Barcelona: Ediciones Destino, 1956).

Funcionario público, eds. Beatrice C. Patt and Martin Nozick (New York: Oxford University Press, 1963).

Nosotros los Rivero (Barcelona: Ediciones Destino, 1953).

El pez sigue flotando (Barcelona: Ediciones Destino, 1959).

2. Novelettes and Short Stories

Andrés (Oviedo: Richard Grandio, 1967).

"Cinco cartas de Alemania," *QP: Revista para los empleados de la Compáñia Telefónica* (April, 1967), pp. 10 12.

"El cochecito de Miguelín," *QP: Revista para los empleados de la Compañia Telefónica* (July, 1970), pp. 10–12.

Compás de espera (Barcelona: Ediciones G.P. [1954]).

Mañana, Cinco novelas. La novela del sábado, V (Madrid: Ediciones Cid, 1954).

El milagro de la Noche de Reyes. (Burgos: Hijos de Santiago Rodríguez, 1948).

"Milagro en Santaolaya," *QP: Revista para los empleados de la Compañía Telefónica* (September, 1971), pp. 10–12.

"Nina." *Cuentistas españolas comtemporáneas* (Madrid: Aguilar, 1946), pp. 375–92.

"Patio de luces," *El español,* No. 291 (June 27–July 3, 1954), pp. 36–42.

"El puñado de yerba seca," *Informaciones* (April 24, 1969), p. 8.

El señor García. La novela popular, No. 33 (Madrid: Alfaguara, 1966).

"Teresa (Solo de recuerdos para un hombre)," *QP: Revista para los empleados de la Compañia Telefónica* (October, 1970), pp. 10–12.

"Tira, Nicolasa. . . . !" *Punta Europa,* 127 (November, 1967), pp. 69–75.

3. Nonfictional Writings

"Aldous Huxley y la novela social (IV)," *Arriba* (November 15, 1964), p. 24.
"Algo sobre el cine infantil." A three-part series published in *Arriba* on the
following dates: November 24, 1963 (pp. 15–16), December 8, 1963
(p. 18), February 2, 1964, (p. 20).
Asturias (Barcelona: Ediciones Destino, 1971).
"Autorretrato-autoentrevista," *La estrafeta literaria,* 77 (January 5, 1957),
p. 5.
"Benavente y la educación," *Arriba* (April 12, 1964), p. 22.
"Comentario en torno a un premio," *Arriba* (December 22, 1963), p. 20.
"Curriculum vitae." n.d. A single printed sheet of biographical information
supplied by the author.
"Démosle al César," *Arriba* (January 12, 1964), p. 22.
"El difícil arte de la entrevista." A two-part article published in *Arriba* on
the following dates: March 1, 1964 (p. 19) and March 15, 1964 (p. 20).
Discurso (Santander: Aldus Velarde, S.A., 1967).
"El escritor y su idioma." Answers to a questionnaire published in *El
urogallo,* No. 2 (April—May 1970), pp. 85–86.
Isabel II de España (Madrid: Editorial Sucesores de Rivadeneyra, 1966).
"Lo autobiográfico en Dostoyewsky," *Arriba* (May 14, 1964), p. 17.
"Lo autobiográfico en la novela," *Arriba* (April 19, 1964), p. 20.
"Lo social en la novela." A series of articles published in *Arriba* on June
28, 1964 (p. 25) and July 12, 1964 (p. 24).
"Lo social en el realismo," *Arriba* (November 22, 1964), p. 21.
"El novelista y sus personajes," *Arriba* (May 24, 1964), p. 22.
"Ortega y la novela objectiva," *Arriba* (December 20, 1964), pp. 22–24.
"Pío Baroja y las mujeres," in *Encuentros con don Pío: Homenaje a Baroja*
(Madrid: Al Borak, [1972?]).
"Psicología y técnica del cuento infantil," *Arriba* (November 17, 1963), p. 20.
Selma Lagerlöf (Madrid: E.P.E.S.A., 1971).
Untitled lecture in *El autor enjuicia su obra* (Madrid: Editora Nacional,
1966).

4. Poetry

"Angustia." Typewritten copy dated 1955.
"El Ataúd." Typewritten copy dated November, 1936.
"El Burro," *ABC,* 1971.
"Cancioncilla del tintero volcado." Typewritten copy dated June, 1936.
"El circo." Typewritten copy dated 1935 or 1936.
"En carne viva." Typewritten copy dated May, 1950.
"Gusanera." Typewritten copy dated November, 1960.
"Idolo." Typewritten copy dated October, 1948.

"Mi calle." Typewritten copy dated 1950.
"Moriré sola." Typewritten copy dated January, 1960.
"Nana," *ABC*, 1971.
"Plegaria." Typewritten copy dated Summer, 1935.
"Rueda de la molinera." Typewritten copy dated Spring, 1936.
"Silencio." Typewritten copy dated January, 1957.

Secondary Sources

ALBORG, JUAN LUIS. *Hora actual de la novela española* (Madrid: Taurus, 1958), II. 333 48. One of the few long analyses of the novels, ends with *Diary of a Schoolteacher*.

ARROITIA-JÁUREGUI, MARCELO. Review of *Nosotros los Rivero*. *Correo Literario* (May 15, 1953), p. 4. An extreme example of the negative criticism that followed the receipt of the Nadal Prize.

CASTILLO-PUCHE, J. L. "Clase media y novela (III): Dolores Medio ha reclutado la casi totalidad de sus personajes en la clase media." *Ya* (June 26, 1965), n.p. Discusses the author's almost exclusive use of the middle class as characters; follows with an interview with Miss Medio on the subject.

DÍAZ, JANET WINECOFF. "Three New Works of Dolores Medio," *Romance Notes*, XI, 2 (Winter, 1969), 244–50. Discusses *Isabel II, Mr. García* and *Andrés*, signaling continuing interests and themes in her production.

DOMINGO, JOSÉ. "Narrativa española," *Insula*, 253 (December, 1967), p. 5. An overview of *Bibiana, Mr. García*, and *Andrés*; emphasizes common interests in the "little man," then places the works in the category of the "social novel."

FERNÁNDEZ DE GUERRERO, ENRIQUETA. "Dolores Medio: *Nosotros los Rivero*," *Revista Nacional de Cultura*, XIV, 99 (July August, 1953), 139–41. A general review, but concentrates on some interesting stylistic aspects.

GARCÍA-LUENGO, EUSEBIO. "Dos novelistas españolas de última hora," *Indice de artes y letras* (October, 1953), n.p. A generally unfavorable review of *We Riveros*, but points also to Miss Medio's excellent talent for describing ordinary everyday events.

GIL CASADO, PABLO. *La novela social española*: Biblioteca breve de bolsillo (Barcelona: Seix Barral, 1968). Places Miss Medio in the group of critical social realists because of *Public Servant*.

GONZÁLEZ, EMILIO. "Dolores Medio: *Nosotros los Rivero*," *Revista hispánica moderna*, XXI, 2 (April, 1955), 150. Points to the importance of society in this work; the place of naturalism in the novel.

HOYOS, ANTONIO DE. *Ocho escritores actuales* (Murcia: Aula de Cultura, 1954), pp. 228–52. Discusses the reaction to *We Riveros*, and analyzes certain aspects of the novel; connects it with the *novela rosa*, then gives background information on "El Aguilucho" (based on an interview with Miss Medio).

MURCIANO, CARLOS. "Dolores Medio, o la experiencia novelada," *Estafeta Literaria*, 408 (November 15, 1969), pp. 8–10. A brief presentation of her works since 1953 with the outstanding elements in each; points to the author's theory of fictionalizing experience.

NORA, EUGENIO G. DE. *La novela española contemporánea (1927–1960)* (Madrid: Editorial Gredos, 1962), II, ii. An indispensable work for an overview of the Spanish novel; divides the novelists into "generations" with like characteristics. Covers the novels through *The Fish Stays Afloat*.

PATT, BEATRICE P. and MARTIN NOZICK. Introduction to Dolores Medio's *Funcionario público* (New York: Oxford University Press, 1963). A brief introduction to Miss Medio's life and works through 1961; in English.

PONCE, FERNANDO. "Dolores Medio en la novela de hoy," *Punta Europa* (November, 1967), pp. 53–58. Emphasis mainly on *We Riveros*.

PRJEVALINSKY FERRER, OLGA. "Las novelistas españolas de hoy," *Cuadernos Americanos,* CXVIII, 5 (September–October, 1961), 211–23. A brief presentation of the outstanding women novelists in Spain; mentions *Nosotros los Rivero*.

REYERO RIAÑO, M. "Dolores Medio, Alumna de la Escuela Superior de Educación de la F.A.E., Premio Nadal, 1952," *Atenas* (February, 1953), pp. 29–31. An interesting section prints an interview with Miss Medio, in which she speaks about heredity and environment as determinants of the personality (as seen in *We Riveros*).

S[AINZ] DE R[OBLES], F[EDERICO] C[ARLOS], "Dolores Medio: *Andrés,*" *Estafeta literaria,* 375 (July 29, 1967), p. 27. A review signaling the similarities among the stories; emphasizes the almost maternal relationship between author and characters; considers it one of her best works.

SORDO, ENRIQUE. "Notas al Margen: *Nosotros los Rivero,*" *Revista Gran Vía de actualidades, arte y letras* (April 30, 1953), p. 11. Praises the novel, signals affinities with Galdós, and mentions the joint use of Oviedo along with Clarín and Pérez de Ayala.

VÁZQUEZ ZAMORA, RAFAEL. "Dolores Medio. De *Nosotros los Rivero* a Ellas, las de la 'Celda Común,'" *Destino* (October 15, 1966), p. 63. An interview with Miss Medio in which she describes her stay in jail in 1962 and announces the literary result of this experience.

VILANOVA, ANTONIO. "*Nosotros los Rivero,* de Dolores Medio," *Destino,* 821 (May 22, 1953), p. 21. An objective review by an excellent critic.

V[ILLA] P[ASTUR], JESÚS]. "Dolores Medio. *Funcionario público,*" *Archivum.* VI, 3 (1956), 383–86. Discusses *We Riveros* and the literary polemic also.

WINECOFF, JANET. "Fictionalized Autobiography in the Novels of Dolores Medio," *Kentucky Foreign Language Quarterly*, XIII, 3 (1966), 170–78. Based on a series of interviews and letters from the novelist, the writer makes a striking case for autobiographical elements in these works.

Index